IMPROVE

YOUR

SOCIAL SKILLS

Stop Anxiety and Build Self-Esteem, Improve Your Social Life, Improve Relationship, Improve Self-Awareness.

Make Friends and Talk to Anyone With High Level Conversation.

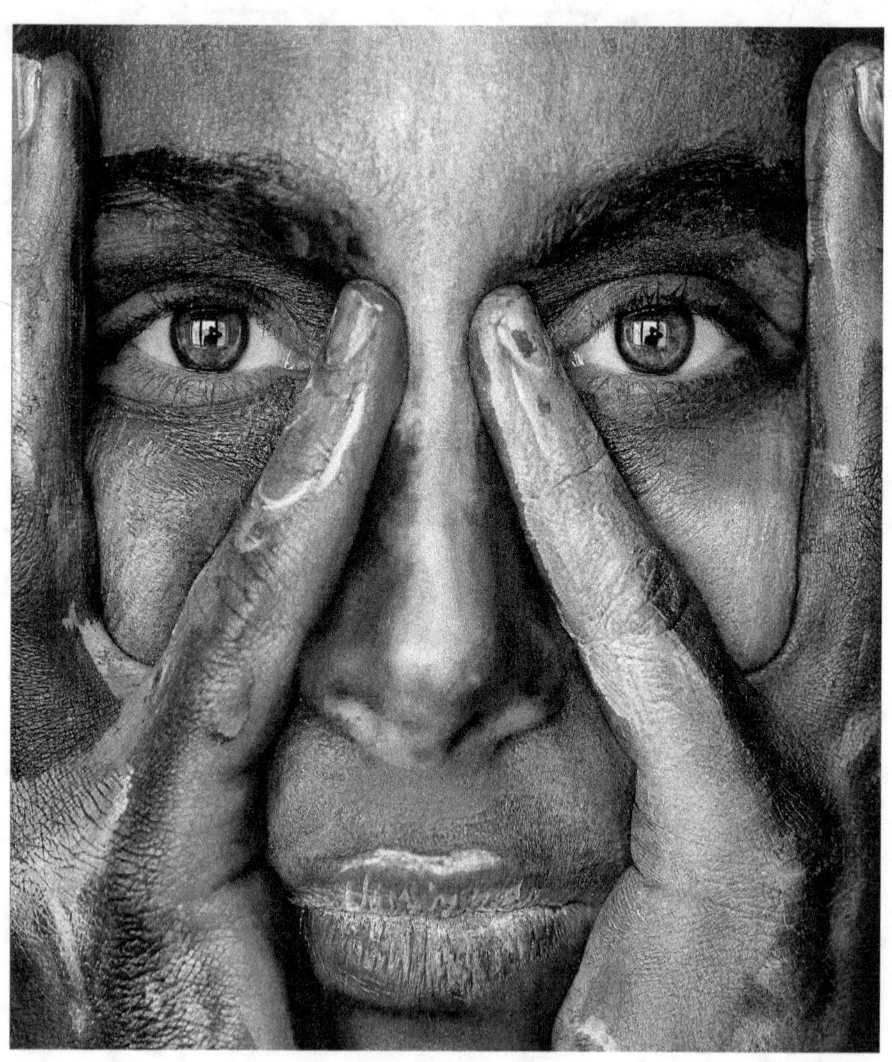

Table of Contents

original author of this work can be in any fashion deemed liable for any hardship or damages that may befall them after undertaking information described herein.

Additionally, the information in the following pages is intended only for informational purposes and should thus be thought of as universal. As befitting its nature, it is presented without assurance regarding its prolonged validity or interim quality. Trademarks that are mentioned are done without written consent and can in no way be considered an endorsement from the trademark holder.

Introduction

Congratulations on purchasing ***"Improve Your Social Skills,"*** and thank you for doing so. It is a social world, and downloading this book is a significant step towards improving your social skills. The first step is usually the easiest. All of the information contained herein is important for you to take to heart. These are not all concepts that you can immediately put into action. However, you can preserve this useful information for use at a later date. Of course, you will find it to be quite educational and worth putting into action in the future.

That being said, the chapters contained in this book will highlight and discuss some steps that are necessary to help you integrate seamlessly into society. This means you will start by learning how to think critically in a social way, and how you can act like a social person by changing your mindset from being antisocial, to an utterly social person. At the same time, you will learn the best way you can put your good manners into action to blend in well with others. Keep in mind that you will have to start gradually while getting integrated into the social circle, as well as adapting to the new environment, among other things.

There are volumes upon volumes of books on how to improve your social skills but thank you once more for selecting this one. Please enjoy!

Chapter 1: Think Socially and Act Like a Social Person

Social skills are more or less the same as any other skill you can learn in your life. This means that if you invest a little of your time and effort in studying and practicing such skills, you will get better as you gain experience. It doesn't matter where you come from, your environment or social status, which is essential in this regard. Anyone can acquire social skills, and it is never too late to do so. That is why your first step into learning social skills should be to think socially and act as a social person. And how do you even get started to achieve this feat?

Think Socially

By nature, humans are social animals. This is evident from their behaviors, beliefs, and desires, which are always affected by the social preferences, their kind of interaction and social contexts that they live in. Human beings have evolved socially to become group-minded individuals who perceive everything in different perspectives. That is why they precisely understand what is in their minds or those around them, and act as though their brains are in sync with those of other people.

However, your ability and tendency to associate with like-minded people who collectively behave in a manner that seems desirable to you shows how you think socially. By associating with members of a group that think almost as you do can lead to affecting the decisions you make as well as your behavior, and this is crucial for your mental development.

Your social tendency as a human being is a clear indication that you are not purely selfish with sharing information and wealth maximization. Your ability to think socially means that you value fairness and reciprocity and that you are more than willing to cooperate in attaining shared goals. In the long run, you will develop a tendency to adhere to a common understanding and principles that will govern your behavior to benefit you or your group of like-minded individuals. After all, what you do will not only have a significant impact on you but also to those you usually interact with. And of course, your influence will change the behavior of everyone within your social circle by simply adopting your social thinking.

But there are consequences of thinking socially. A necessary result is, different groups comprising of like-minded people and even the societies across the board can adopt, and sadly stick to a particular collective pattern of behavior, such as segregation, corruption, supremacism and civil wars, that arguably benefit no one in particular.

On the other hand, the same tactics of social thinking can have a significant impact. Similar to social behavior, temporary interventions can lead to having a broad and everlasting positive outcome on a specific community through the shift in the pattern of social interactions. Also, social thinking can act as a lever for different types of development intervention that are likely going to harness the tendencies of individual groups to look for social status, maintain social identities and improve cooperation with other people under certain conditions. All these attributes come about when you or those within your group think socially, to develop your social skills.

There is an innate human desire for tendencies to be identified with certain groups and help one another in acquiring new social status and propensities to identify themselves with other people who are ready and willing to cooperate with them. As a human being, you can take full advantage of such desires and tendencies to advance your social skills by interacting with other people within your social network. This is because social networks play a crucial role in transmitting social influence to spur social change.

In addition to that, social networks are known to provide the right platforms where you will learn and adopt essential skills that can help you think socially. And one thing that will help you to realize such changes, is what is commonly referred to as social norms. Through social norms, you will be able to coordinate your behavior and adopt new principles that will guide you all along as you interact with others.

Just like a river flowing through a specific society, so is the human sociality. Its impact on the community is immeasurable, given that it influences everyone, shapes individuals, and helps them pursue a common goal in their daily undertakings. Now that you are part and parcel of that society, you can choose to follow the current or swim upstream but know that whichever decision you make it will have a positive or a negative impact in the end. For that reason, sociability will serve as a stepping stone to the new world of development interventions through which your social skills will play a very significant role.

One area that can help you tap into your potential in improving your social skills, lies in social networks. Although getting into search networks is an individual's decision, there is no better way of learning how to think socially than through a social network. As the world changes technologically, human beings are shifting from the traditional way of doing things to the modern way of life. This doesn't imply that these changes affect a handful of people but a multitude from different corners of the world.

The truth of the matter is that all of us are embedded in all kinds of networks that suit our needs. Of course, these are networks of our social relations that are tailored towards shaping our resources, beliefs, preferences, and choices we make in our daily lives. After some time, you will come to the full realization that any social network is a set of actors as well as relational ties, forming the very building blocks of your social experience. Why is the case?

The answer is simple and clear. Networks are essential platforms that provide different scopes with which individuals can reinforce existing human behavior among themselves. At the same time, these networks can help them in transmitting normative pressures and novel information that, at some point, will spark social change as a result of thinking socially. Apart from that, the ability of a social network to both shift and stabilize patterns of people's behavior indicate that they may play an essential role in their social settings in which formal institutions are not available.

Unfortunately, most people disregard social networks even though these are a foundational basis of any social order. And without a warrant, human beings can be rendered savages in all aspects of their behavior and how they relate to one another. So, socially thinking can overcome such negative human attributes and make the world a better place for everyone.

Socially thinking will help you blend in perfectly with people from different backgrounds and social status. Your sociability will enable you to break barriers and get influenced by new ideas coming from your social peers.

It will be a matter of time before you get to realize the importance of thinking collectively and sharing ideas that are constructive in the long run. On the other hand, selfishly acting will lock you out of many available opportunities.

It is evident that human behavior is diverse, and everyone chooses what is appropriate for them. But being antisocial or introvert can be a choice that will limit your social skills and deny you a golden opportunity to learn and share vital information with others. While some individuals come out to defend the idea of being anti-social, the ramifications of this vice outweigh the benefits in a social setup. It doesn't mean that the society is forcing you to adopt those ideas and norms that could go against your well-being, but it is only encouraging you to start thinking socially in order have a positive impact on your social skills.

It is true you that you may experience some negativities on your quest to acquiring the right social skills, but it doesn't mean you fall out along the way. When the going gets tough, the tough get going, and you need to overcome every barrier if you want to realize your potential. Nothing comes the easy way, but through persistence, you will understand how easy you will get to achieve your goals. Therefore, the first step to start improving your social skills lies in your ability to start thinking socially. In this way, your mind will be prepared adequately for what lies in the future, and by the time you reach the peak of all events, you will be in a better position to showcase your social ability.

But keep in mind that you cannot do it on your own unless you interact with individuals with whom you share common interests and are eager to learn from each other. Socially thinking means that you will soon start acting socially and return; your social skills will be on an entirely new level.

Be comfortable with all strata of society

A socially skilled person can get along with people across all strata of society. Not necessarily every person, but every type of person. This is a useful skill, and it is also a significant benchmark. You could rely on commonality with a clone of yourself but must genuinely exercise your social skills when trying to relate to someone with whom you have little in common. If you cannot do that, then you may be skilled at relating to people with whom you are compatible with, but not be socially competent.

The commonality is a shortcut to rapport, and a good one to use if it is available. But sometimes the most interesting conversations and friendships happen between people with little commonality. After all, by definition, if you have less in common, there's more new territory to explore.

Building this skill requires travel outside of one's comfort zone, as well as grappling with hidden insecurity. On one end of the spectrum, it's possible to feel inferior to people you admire, as though you don't have any value to add to the relationship. On both ends, lack of commonality can be a hard barrier to cross, especially if it is apparent that you're from different backgrounds and the other person is intimidated by it.

Someone who is comfortable interacting and befriending people in all strata of society will feel comfortable in nearly every situation, confident in his ability to add to any interaction of which he's a part. He'll have more opportunities to share what he knows with others, as well as the ability to learn from experiences that he may never have personally.

Be a net addition

Beyond just getting along with people in all strata of society, you want to generally be a net positive to any social situation in which you're placed. If someone was eating alone, and you were to join them, that should make their lunch better. If a few friends are having tea together, and you get invited, your presence should make everyone have a better time. And if you go to a large party or event, even though your impact will be proportionally smaller due to the size, those you interact with should be glad that you were at the party.

Most social circles are a series of concentric circles. There's the small inner nucleus of people who organize and get invited to everything, and without whom events wouldn't even happen. Then there's the next ring of people who are always welcome but would never displace a member of the nucleus. Outside of those two circles are people who usually get invited, but only if space permits. Or maybe they have specific personality quirks that make them incompatible with others in that circle, meaning the core group must choose who gets invited and who doesn't.

The nucleus is comprised of the people who are net additions, and who orchestrate events. The next circle is those who are also new additions. The circle further out are people who are "not negative." Sometimes they add, sometimes they're neutral. They're nice to have around, but not a, sure enough, the thing to make sure they come to every event. Beyond those rings are people who are sometimes or always net negatives.

By ensuring that you're always a net addition, even if you're not a huge one, you will dramatically increase the number of events to which you are invited. Besides being fun and valuable, these invitations will provide you with events at which you can practice your social skills, creating a virtuous.

Being dynamic

I probably shouldn't say this, as it will make just about everyone feel awkward around me, but I'm continually analyzing people's social skills. When I really like being around someone, I think a lot about why that so. There are some people whom I can spend weeks with and still be excited about their company. How do they do that?

The real mysteries, though, are the people who I should like spending time with, but just don't. They're good people, don't rub me the wrong way at all, and yet I can take or leave them; as I see who gets invited to what, I often notice that others feel the same way.

What do these people have in common? What can they do to shift the perception others have of them and be in a better position to share their positive aspects?

The best definition, loose as it is, is that these people lack the quality of being dynamic. They're predictable, reserved, and seem to endeavor to minimize their impact on others.

In my definition, I mean a particular type of being predictable. It's good to be predictably timely, cheerful, and any other number of positive attributes. But there's something really magnetic about someone who brings something different to the interaction every time. You don't know what they'll say. Maybe they'll have a fascinating question they're mulling over, perhaps a great new story, or maybe some exciting new place they've found. Their positive contribution to social interaction is unpredictable.

People who are reserved and minimize their impact succeed in leaving everyone unoffended, but people go to social gatherings for a reason, and that reason is not to be unoffended or remain un-impacted.

Act Like a Social Person

You don't need some form of magic or a Ph.D. in rocket science to act as a social person. It all starts with you before getting influenced by other like-minded people. In this regard, your ability to think socially should motivate you to act like a social person if at all, you are ready to hone your social skills. And if you do it right soon or later, you will be on everyone's minds, and your sociability will pave the way to a world of opportunities.

You may get despaired or face some negativity from pessimists, but your courage and resilience will pay off ten-fold. You can start from a simple conversation with strangers to several chats to those who try to talk you all the way taking part in team-work activities among others. All these actions are meant to make you seem like a social person, and within no time, you will be one. So, let's find a way out to make your life quite enjoyable through acting as a social person.

Initiate a constructive conversation with a stranger(s)

Taking the initiative to strike up a conversation requires enough courage and some wisdom because you are not sure of the response from the other party. But whatever the outcome, you should be fully prepared no matter what. However, your approach will lay a firm foundation for your conversation. A good strategy will lead to a meaningful discussion, but an immature one might culminate into an unpleasant situation that will leave you despaired or embarrassed all along. So, where do you start?

Greetings are known to break all barriers among different people and society's world over. Greetings are a sign of peace, friendliness, politeness, and good manners. Walk straight to your target audience and say "hello, nice meeting you and I are so and so…"

Even though the person you are trying to have a conversation with doesn't show signs of being interested in the first place, greetings will ultimately change that. If you are lucky enough, your discussion will mark the beginning of a very long relationship and a social network.

By the time you finish with greetings, you should know what comes next if at all, your intention is to initiate and maintain that particular conversation. Of course, you will introduce yourself formally, and by doing so, the tension between you and your immediate target will gradually start going down. This is the right time to break the ice and introduce the topic of your discussion.

It may sound easier said than done, but if you are well versed with what is happening around you, you will not fail to find a topic that both of you will enjoy discussing. You can think of sports, climate change, current affairs, or even politics if only you share a common approach on that.

Make your conversation an interesting one and let your new partner keep enjoying everything you say to stay relevant while gradually gaining more and more confidence. With time your friendly approach and ability to sustain a conversation will motivate you into talking to different people regardless of their social status, beliefs, age differences, culture, and background. A good discussion will create an everlasting impression to those you closely interact with, and in the end, you will suddenly come to realize that your social skills are paying off day by day and from person to person.

Chat back to those who try to talk to you

Perhaps at one point, you might have tried talking to individuals you've just run into and they coldly respond to by their one-word response. For sure this sounds rude and paints you as someone out there to intrude others. Such unfortunate encounters are enough to discourage you, especially when it is your first time to try to engage someone in a conversation.

If other people around are trying to initiate a chat with you, it is polite of you to make an effort by giving them positive and meaningful responses in return. It won't cost you a thing, but you will stand to gain even more through that simple gesture. Besides, your social skills will improve significantly by learning how to handle different people in different situations verbally. Being selfish and self-centered will not help you in any way, and you will stand to lose a lot of good chances or opportunities if you have that terrible habit of snubbing other people.

Take part in various group activities

There are numerous activities taking place around, and you can take a while from your busy schedule to participate in them. This is one area that you can sharpen your social skills through close interaction with people from different places and diverse backgrounds. Being part of an active group means that you and other members will spend much of your time discussing, issuing instructions, or giving suggestions where necessary. Doing so will help you in learning effective ways to communicate with your peers.

On the other hand, you may invite your friends, neighbors, family members, and even strangers to be part of your forthcoming event. It could be your birthday party, your wedding or even your fundraising event. At the height of your event, you will have that opportunity to express yourself, and there's no better way of doing so if not that your communication and social skills are top notches. It doesn't mean that you have to be a good speaker or crown mobilizer, but you can gradually learn as time goes by.

Try to look like an outgoing person

Who doesn't like associating with celebrities? Of course, everyone wishes to be in the shoes of their favorite celebrities for one reason or the other. This is not to imply that you have to break your back, trying vehemently to look and behave like someone famous. What it means is that you need to look and act in a manner that will portray you as someone outgoing. And the best way to do so is through your social skills.

Being an outgoing person will give you enough confidence to face different people without fear of being intimidated or ridiculed, given that nearly all your friendly status will place you in a position almost similar to that of a celebrity. Now that you will be accorded such status, it will be upon you to take advantage of your near-celebrity status to improve your social skills. It may not be easy for you to attain such status overnight, but through self-determination and hard work, nothing will stand your way.

Join other people where they are

They could be your workmates, family members or your fellow students you want to establish a close link with them. Ensure that you join them wherever they go and in what they are doing. If it is a lunch-hour or an evening stroll, you should always consider being part of that group so you may learn how to socialize with different people.

For instance, if you happen to be at a party, and almost everyone is talking at the front porch, compose yourself and join them to take part in what they might be discussing. Share your views on the topic of discussion and be ready to listen to others. Keeping to yourself will not do you any kind rather than denying you the chance to practice your social skills.

Even though being an introvert is not harmful in any way, it might look awkward to keep to yourself at a social gathering when everyone is jovial and to share one or two jokes. You will look out of place and consequently, get bored all along. Therefore, find the best way to approach other people and use that opportunity to improve your social skills.

Spend some time with people

It is always important to spend some time with people as you learn their way of life and how they carry on with their activities. These could be your friends, neighbors or even workmates. Give them your quality time, and they will appreciate your effort in doing so.

Giving people much of your time should not be taken as a waste of your precious moment because every person you come across will influence you either positively or negatively. Whichever the case, it is upon you to make up your mind on what you are being impacted on.

As you spend more time with people, you will likely come across someone who will help you in changing the way you approach and socialize with others. Also, it will help you to learn better ways of handling different types of people given that every society has its uniqueness, so are its people. If your social skills are improving, it merely means that you are on the right track.

Thinking socially and acting as a social person is one step into the realms of a social world. Since no man is an island, it means that we need each other to survive, to share our happiness, triumph, sadness, story and even our achievements. There is no better way human beings can express themselves if not through socializing; hence the need to improve on our social skills. Therefore, start by thinking socially and acting like a social person and the world around you will be a better place to express yourself freely.

Chapter 2: Learn and Apply Good Manners to Improve Your Social Skills

"Manners maketh man" is a famous quote from the movie, *'Kingsman: The Secret Service,"* and it merely means that their manners judge human beings. Without good manners, then the rest of humanity is savagery. Every society, individuals, and different institutions across the world will treat you according to your behaviors, let alone your physical appearance. Learning and applying good manners should be the first thing to do if you want to have a positive impact on your social skills.

The importance of having outstanding social skills cannot be overlooked right in the earliest years of childhood to a complete adult. Solid social skills play a very crucial role in shaping an individual as well as helping with personal relationships and career advancement.

There are many ways you can improve your social skills, and one of them is through learning and adopting good manners that will make you be accepted in society. From the basics of good manners to group activities, all the way to help bolster skills. If need be, you may seek outside assistance from professionals who will help establish a firm foundation for what is coming ahead of you.

Explain Your Personal Space

One of the basics that you will need when learning good manners is to explain your own space. This is essential in helping you grasp the concept that those you will interact with, in the near future, have their space bubble, and they deserve respect from you.

To understand this concept fully, you will need to keep at the back of your mind that personal space varies from one individual to the next and from one culture to another. It will be upon you to take your time to understand those people who are closer to you. They could be your relatives, friends, school mates, parents, and your siblings.

For example, one group of individuals may be more comfortable with the idea of hugging and touching while the rest are used to just shaking hands and a simple peck on their cheeks or hands. This is because any given society comprises of different people and different cultures; thus the need to learn how you can approach everyone. In other words, some people may have varied preferences for personal space.

Still, on the personal space, you will need to go an extra mile to study everyone's body language keenly. Though it may sound like a complicated thing to learn, a body language is universal, and with the right knowledge about it, you can always interpret it from one person to the other.

The first signs you will have to look out for in a person you are trying to interact with will tell you if that particular person is interested or not. For instance, you may have come across a group of people or just an individual who portrays a sign of tensing up or crossing their arms and eventually backing away. This is a clear sign that you are infringing on their personal space, and they are uncomfortable about it. So, if you had prior knowledge of body language, you would not try to invade their space in the first place.

Likewise, you are also entitled to your personal space. And once you are pretty sure of this fact, you will not let anyone get into your space without your permission. Don't just let anyone hug you without your consent in the same way you wouldn't embrace other people without consenting to that idea. Just know that you have full authority over your own body in the same way as other people.

Understand the Necessary Skills to Have a Good Conversation

If you have basic conversational skills, know that you are on the right path to social development. But for someone trying to learn good manners and applying them in a standard setup, this can be a daunting task. To begin with, you may not have any idea of where to start, and you will be likely to be prone to interrupting others in the middle of their conversation. On one side, you might be lacking the right skills to initiate a conversation between you and a stranger or those within your social circle.

However, you should not be worried anymore if your social skills are way below your expectations. Everything has a beginning, and from here, you will have basic ideas on how you can have good manners that will help you sharpen your social skills.

Almost all interactive moments start from somewhere, leading to something more meaningful and long-lasting. That is why you will begin by learning how to enter a conversation without interrupting others or appearing like an unwanted guest.

The first thing that you will need to do is to start with basic greetings. Greetings are known to be the first show of respect when you are about to engage a stranger in a conversation. Addresses break that barrier that generally exists between two groups of strangers and creates the first impression that other people will use to gauge your social manners.

A simple 'hi' or "How are you" can change the whole game, and you could be on your way to establishing a long lasting relationship with people you always perceive to be strangers. Or you can think of using non-verbal cues if you are not sure of the language to use when initiating that very first move in a conversation. You can start by nodding, waving, smiling and handshaking. Well, a handshake has been known to be the most effective form of nonverbal greeting, and it serves the purpose of easing the tension between you and the next person.

Listening and waiting for the other person to speak is a vital skill that you will need to hold a meaningful conversation. Looking at someone without interrupting their conversation is a show of respect and being interested in what is being discussed. But interjecting when someone is speaking can make you look disrespectful, especially when having a conversation with a stranger for the first time.

Learning to be assertive while having a conversation with someone is one of the best skills that can improve your sociability. To be assertive does not imply that you are aggressive, but it means you are making an inquiry of what you want your subject to respond directly and honestly. When you communicate assertively, you should not use insults, threats or excuses to drive your point home. Stick to your ethical principles and use a polite language with a friendly tone throughout your conversation.

Acquire Basic Manners

By now, you are old enough to understand good manners in general. However, you need to learn some basic behaviors that you can use to enhance your social skills. Using common phrases like thank you, please, excuse me, and all other forms of common courtesy can influence the way you interact with other people. Make these phrases to be part and parcel of your conversation as a way to convey good manners to those around you. Once this becomes a habit in your speech or communication, you will eventually come to realize how polished your social skills have grown. As the saying goes, "practice makes perfect," and you may capitalize on that if you want to stay in the game.

Basic manners don't just limit you to use polite words or phrases but go as far as employing the use of other equally critical social skills. One of the best skills that show how honest or interested you are in a conversation is the use of eye contact. It is understandable that there are shy people, and you could be one of them but maintaining eye contact with your subject will install a sense of confidence in you while making your conversation worthwhile.

Learning and adopting good manners goes beyond holding a constructive conversation with someone. Remember, table manners are also part of your social skills and one of the best etiquettes at meal time. Good behavior will make you stand out among the rest, and everyone will want to associate with you all the time. Before taking meals, especially when you are a guest, it is prudent that you start with observing your hygiene. Wash your hands thoroughly before meals, don't speak in between mouthfuls, place your napkin on your lap, use polite language and gestures while at the table with other guests and always remember to clear your dishes from the dining table.

Patience is not common among individuals, but it is also part of basic manners. Being impatience with others will not go down well, and you may end up being snubbed, or your presence assumed completely. Of course, you will not take it in kind if others treat you in a manner that will lower self-esteem. To avoid such awkward moments in a social gathering, practice patience and tolerance and learn what others expect from you so that your interaction with them will run smoothly. In addition to that, showing some elements of indulgence to your friends and family members will mean that you care and consider others in what you do. This is because human beings are a unique lot, and their reactions to different social situations might not be the same.

Eliminating Annoyance

Before you begin working on how to bring a lot to the table, as a friend and a member of a friend group, it is essential to work on eliminating behaviors which annoy. None of us will ultimately succeed in removing all our annoying behaviors, but there's a certain threshold that must be crossed for people with other good options to choose you as a friend.

This is a harsh thing to say, but that doesn't make it untrue. Some of those you will most want to become friends with will already have a ton of good friends who are all competing for their time. If you have annoying habits, there's no guarantee that a new friend or acquaintance will be able to see past those habits and discover the great things about you.

A classic example is talking too much about things that the other person isn't interested in. There are guidelines to follow on how much of the conversation should be you listening versus you speaking, but in general volume alone won't make or break an interaction. After all, even if you prefer being the one to talk, if

I'm revealing interesting discoveries about subjects that matter to you, you're unlikely to want me to stop.

But if I'm talking about my ambitions as a marathoner, and you have no interest in running, your capacity to enjoyably listen to me is limited.

Another common annoying habit is making bad jokes. No one thinks that they make bad jokes, but everyone knows some people that do, so there's an apparent disconnect. Some people consistently make bad jokes and don't realize it. You might be one of these people.

Both of these are undesirable traits, not because you're malicious or because they imply something wrong about you, but because they create an unnecessary imposition on the other person, and require him to either deceive you or be rude.

If you talk too much to me about subjects in which I have no interest, I must be polite, listen, and feign interest. The only alternative is for me to be rude, either by changing the subject as abruptly as I can manage or by telling you I'm not interested. Some people are so oblivious about overtaking that they won't pick up on any subtle cues make you aware that your jokes aren't funny. In either scenario, you've placed an awkward imposition upon me, making me less comfortable, less interested in the conversation, and more motivated to exit.

Identifying annoying habits is more difficult than eliminating them. Often awareness creates enough social pressure to at least dampen the annoying habit. If you have a friend or family member who is willing to be completely honest with you, you can ask them what annoying habits you have. Don't ask if you have any, assume that you do, and ask what they are. This saves your friend the awkward step of revealing to you that you have some.

Think about how often you'd be wrong when pointing out someone else's annoying habit. Probably rarely to never, so when someone gives you that sort of feedback, assume that they are correct.

You will have to find some annoying habits on your own, though. The biggest red flag is when you are consistently getting reactions that differ from those you expect. You make a joke, and the laughter is muted. You talk about something that interesting to you, but you see eyes wander and notice that your listeners don't ask any clarifying questions.

These are just two examples of many. Others include overuse of certain words, unnecessary hand gestures, not making eye contact, and not listening.

Take Your Interest in Any Activity that Promotes Social Skills

A great way to help you model your social skills is by developing an interest in any action that is likely to encourage social behavior. There are hundreds of activities that you may engage in to improve your social skills. One of them is taking part in games where you will meet different people learn one or more things from each other. Games or sports bring people together, and this is one area to achieve scores of people with whom you probably share a common interest. If you are not a social person, taking part in such activities will change your social life as well as your perspective about other people.

Apart from that, you can also look further and reach out to those games that are explicitly designed to encourage conversations regarding social skills. Through such games, you will sharpen your conversational skills as well as your analytical thinking. This is one area you should consider given that it will expose you to various activities that will compel you y to engage other people in a one-on-one conversation. In the end, your shyness and introvert behavior will drastically change to something more meaningful.

According to the research, critical social skills such as leadership and empathy are usually learned during participation in various games. This means that when you show an interest in a specific game, you will need to find a way to be part of it. These games will have a positive impact on your overall social skills, besides engaging in physical activities to keep you healthy, both physically and mentally. The same research suggests that those people who start participating in team sports are less likely to abuse harmful substances and that they stand a good chance of having better self-esteem. However, you should not limit all your thoughts to sports even if your interest is not there. There are hundreds upon hundreds of other activities that can help you realize your potential in various fields of endeavor with social skills being one of them.

Other activities that can transform you into a social person include religious gatherings, picnics, going out to a club or an event with friends, and taking part in voluntary services within your residential areas. All these activities will make you meet many people, and you will not miss out on establishing some friendship with a couple of them in the course of your interaction.

Seek External Support, if Necessary

It is not a bad idea to go looking for outside assistance in a bid to improve your social skills. This is necessary because at one point in your life, you will realize that you need to establish a close relationship with others to experience mutual benefit. As stated earlier, human beings are different, and their way of developing varies from one individual to the other. Some people have no problem with acquiring necessary social skills while others find it quite taxing to socialize with those around them. Since we are all in a typical setup, it will be awkward to lack basic skills that will enable you to mingle with others.

But there comes a time when your social development is way below your age mates, and however much you try to acquire those skills, nothing comes your way. Maybe your inability to develop socially is a sign that there is something different about you hence the need for some intervention. It could be some conditions such as autism or genetic disabilities that are hindering you from becoming a complete person in a given social setup.

It doesn't mean that you sit back and accept your fate as it is, but you can find an immediate remedy to help you lead a normal life. Seek advice and help from a psychiatrist if you are finding it hard to get along with others or not being able to recognize pictures or figures of familiar objects and so on. All these could be signs of someone whose social development is slow, or it is happening at an uneven pace. Accessing the right help in time can save you the agony of being in perpetual isolation.

Look for a Mentor

There are many ways you can nurture your manners with the aim of improving your social skills. Since human beings learn from each other, it will be a sound idea to look for someone who will help you in nurturing your manners towards attaining proper and well-polished social skills. Having a good mentor around you will significantly impact your social behavior by copying and applying what your mentors teach you. Most people feel appreciated whenever they get someone to hold their hand and guide them in the right direction. When coupled with a positive attitude, you will undoubtedly be surprised how fast you will start catching up with every step your mentor helps to undertake. But remember your will-power to learn, adapt, and apply good manners is the only factor that will determine your social behavior.

Another important thing about having a mentor beside you is that you will get some encouragement, and giving up along the way will not be an option for you. When reinforced with valuable teaching tools, you will not have to spend more time grasping one or two concepts that you will need to apply to change the course of your social behavior.

A good mentor means a lot when it comes to transforming someone from being anti-social or clueless about interacting with others to being an all-round extrovert who can fit in any society perfectly. With a seasoned mentor on good manners that can help you improve your social skills, you will be at a more significant advantage of learning admirable traits such as helpfulness, kindness, cooperation, politeness, patience, honesty, altruism, consideration, compassion, empathy, graciousness and gentleness. If you can attain a handful of such traits, there will be no society that you won't fit in unless it is a hostile one. All these traits are geared towards making you a complete person full of attributes that others will find desirable. When combined, all these traits will give you essential skills to participate comfortably in any activity within your community and beyond.

Master the Art of Social Dynamics

Mastering the art of social dynamics entails quite a lot of steps when learning how to behave when applying good manners. First of all, you will need to start by building the knowledge, the like and the trust factor with your colleagues, potential friends, clients and even your boss (if you are in a work environment). The art of social dynamism should help you to conquer all available networks by applying a better strategy that will take you from one stage to the next. To achieve that feat, you will have to master your conversations to appear competent and intelligent during your interaction with like-minded individuals.

By mastering the art of social dynamics, you will be setting a good platform that will enable you to maneuver your way into different groups of people with ease. This is not possible unless you have acquired basic manners that you can apply in any situation to blend in well with others. In the real sense, social dynamics will keep you on the right track and ahead of the game when it comes to associating with all types of people.

In a nutshell, your good manners will always create the first impression of you whenever you meet and have a conversation with new people. Your physical appearance may play a role, but not as much as your manners and everyone will judge you based on that. Sadly we all live in a judgmental world, and everyone you will come into contact with will judge you according to your deeds. Of course, nothing brings forth our acts better if not through the way we behave. Our behavior is the sole determinant of who we are and how we are treated. There are countless ways that you can learn good social manners. All these include; explaining your personal space, acquiring basic manners, showing particular interest in those activities that promote social skills, seeking to help from a mentor to mastering the art of social dynamics. These are some of the best ways that you can learn how to carry yourself when interacting with others at any common setup. Therefore, learning and applying good manners should be one of the vital steps that you can take to improve your social skills.

Chapter 3: Start off Gradually to Acquire Social Skills

Everything has a starting point, so does your quest to improve your social skills. The truth of the matter is that no one was born with all the necessary social skills. Since life is a learning process, most of those you perceive to be socially endowed started from somewhere and grew to master these vital skills at their different stages of development.

Being of a certain age does not imply that you cannot start gradually and become a pro in socializing. Just give yourself some hope knowing that it is never too late to achieve your dreams. What you need is self-determination, the will power and the right platform on which you will launch your campaign to transform from being an introvert to a social person. So, where do you even get started?

Naturally, those perceived to be social didn't just wake up and found their way at the top of the social pyramid. They started from somewhere building up their confidence and social skills gradually. However, there are various places you can frequent in your free time to learn one or two tricks that can help you become a complete social person. These places include clubs, bars, restaurants, parties, public functions, schools, colleges and even religious gatherings, among others. Different people choose places that suit them or make them feel comfortable when mingling with others. What is essential in this regard is determining what works well for you.

Some people think that we are evolutionarily hardwired to evade situations with many strangers for safety reasons. While this notion is correct, it doesn't mean that we cannot approach strangers to establish a long-standing relationship. You can only know how social you are by mingling with people you hardly know and striking a constructive conversation. That is what makes other people look naturally social as compared to others. And that leads us to look critically into what it entails to be a typically socially successful person. Perhaps you are one of those lucky few to be social, but you are not yet sure about yourself. If you are not, you will consider looking for a conducive environment where you will feel comfortable in any social situation. In the actual sense, such an environment will help you to recreate the social path that will eventually lead you to other new avenues.

It will not surprise you to realize that the person with whom you perceive to be outgoing started right from kindergarten. As the years went by, the person in question nurtured the right skills, both communication and interactive, to become naturally socially. You too can identify the right spot to pitch your tent and work from nothing to something as far as becoming a social person entails. All that you need to do is have courage, the will, and determination, and everything will work in your favor.

This can sound obvious to you when presented this way, but upon seeing socially successful people interacting with others might not look that simple and obvious. Of course, you will feel disillusioned and then decide to give up prematurely. But before you call it to quit, always remember that fortune favors the bold. Be courageous and face any obstacle that might come your way. Don't dwell on an unsubstantiated belief that some people are born to be more successful than others. Nature does not allow that unless there is some amount of hard work involved. Therefore, every time you see a socially successful person in action, try to imagine the amount of effort and time they invested in achieving their target. You too can be like them only if you gather your courage and face any challenges coming your way.

On the other hand, it is essential to have an idea of the process involved when building social skills as well as confidence. Just in the same way, those socially successful people worked so hard to attain their current status, so should you. If others can do it, you too have what it takes to do it even better.

Start gradually by discovering those social situations that you think are a little bit thrilling but are still worth the struggle. Sit back and draw a plan that will guide you to overcome those thrills in whatever social situation you find yourself in. For example, you are used to enjoying parties in a company of a good friend that you have full trust in. But in the absence of your friend, the situation gets different directly because you cannot compose yourself and face strangers or mingle with people you do not know. To emerge a socially endowed person, you might consider taking the bull by the horns and face the situation as it comes.

One beautiful evening you can choose to attend the party on your own in the absence of your closest friend and see how things will unfold for you. That will be the right moment to unleash your potential and overcome your fears. You never know the outcome, but with the right attitude and overcoming your concerns, you may find it quite easy to socialize with others without necessarily looking upon your friend to give you some courage. That is one way of starting to improve your social skills. Don't stop there and feel that you have finally achieved your dream. Just keep in your mind that there is more to come hence the need to be fully prepared.

Another perfect example is joining a meetup or a club for what you enjoy doing. Maybe it could be a meetup with your fellow entrepreneurs or athletes with a common interest in enhancing your talent. Take advantage of such meetings to further your social skills. Let others see you as an active person through your full participation in crucial matters affecting your organization or team and give suggestions where necessary.

In the actual sense, doing so will make profound differences between changing your current situation to become who you wish to be and forever remaining the same. As time passes by, these situations will gradually start feeling more natural, leading you to take entirely new steps. This doesn't mean that your task is already accomplished, but it instead gives you an excellent platform to advance your social skills.

Levels of Communication

The cable that comes into your home for TV has only two wires running through it. The cable itself is a fundamental piece of technology that can be understood by anyone. But through this simple medium, hundreds of channels, as well as access to the entire internet, are transmitted. A lot is happening simultaneously.

This is very similar to how we communicate. Our words may seem very simple, but there are several different channels of communication being transmitted at the same time. To master social skills, you must be aware of these channels, be able to communicate effectively on them, and be able to understand what is being transmitted to you over them.

Four main channels are being communicated on at all times: content, Meta, emotion, and status.

Content is what we think of when we talk about communication superficially. If you tell me that you're going to the store, the content channel is merely telling me that you are going to travel to the store.

The meta-channel is the undercurrent of the conversation. It's the meaning behind the meaning-- the implication. If we had been talking about how I wanted to eat brownies, and you're going to the store, the meta-channel communication is that you're going to get ingredients to make me brownies. Sometimes Meta can be read in isolation, but it usually requires context.

The emotion channel is more of a passive signal than an active circuit. Those of us who are not expert poker players are continuously leaking out our emotions as we speak. You could say, "I'm going to the store" in any number of tones and cadences. You could indicate that you were going to the store in resignation because I wouldn't stop hounding you about making me brownies. You could suggest that you loved me, and that's why you were going to get ingredients to make me brownies.

You could also reveal that you were frustrated, nervous, excited, or any other number of emotions.

And last, the status channel is continually sending out clues about our relative status. If I were your boss and told you to go make brownies, you could say, "I'm going to the store" as an affirmation that you understood my command, and we're going to comply with it. You could also say it in a condescending tone that indicates that you're going to do it because I'm so far below you that I'm incapable of doing such an essential task myself.

I'm going to the store. Five essential words, chosen at random that could mean just about anything, even though the content doesn't change. If you weren't already awed at the power of communication, this might do it. It is incredible how much can be conveyed simultaneously.

A master of communication must be able to have two meaningful conversations (content and Meta) while maintaining two minor conversations (emotion and status). This is no exaggeration. If someone were to transcribe the Meta conversation between you and another person, it should be coherent. Same with the other two. If that conversation did not flow as smoothly as the content channel, you'd find that the conversation was frustrating to one or both of you, even if you couldn't identify why.

Each channel has its strengths and weaknesses, so when it's vital to convey something, you need to choose the right channel to focus on. I'll spare you a discussion on the content channel since you're able to understand it if you're able to read this book, but the other three channels deserve individual attention, especially since the most critical aspects of conversation happen in the channels hidden behind the content channel.

Meta

The meta-channel may be the most important of the four. It's where real discussions happen. Sometimes you intentionally communicate incorrect information on the content channel, through sarcasm or joking, allowing your real message to come through on Meta.

The critical thing to understand about the meta-channel is that it's running all the time. People you speak with will always be wondering what you mean.

Let's say that you suggested that a group eat pizza. A couple of people agree to do so, and then another person says, "I guess I could do pizza." What he's communicating on the meta-channel is that he is willing to conform to group consensus and eat pizza, but that he'd rather eat somewhere else.

Now people answering after him can take that information into account when forming their responses. If the next person says, "Pizza sounds good," he's communicating a strong preference for pizza. He's ignoring the meta-message from the previous person. If he were less interested in pizza, the Meta communication from the previous person gave him the opportunity to begin shifting opinion. He could have said, "I could do pizza, or something else."

Once everyone answers, you have a good idea of how everyone in the group feels about it, but you still have options. If people hesitantly agreed and communicated on the meta-channel that they'd instead go somewhere else, you could have switched plans.

You might wonder what the point of this all is, especially if you're a very logical person. Indeed, it would be easier to communicate facts in the content channel and have no meta-channel.

The point of the meta-channel is that it allows for shades of gray not afforded by the content channel. If the content channel is a lecture, the meta-channel is a dance. It's pushing and pulling, circling and parrying. Imagine if someone said, "I'll eat at the pizza place, but I'd rather go somewhere else." That's what our first-person precisely communicated on Meta, but when it's in the content channel, it means something different. It's a much stronger disagreement and is the beginning of a disharmonious decision-making process.

Communicating on the meta-channel also allows people to save face. Let's say you met someone and liked them. They said that they want to see a Vermeer exhibit at a local museum. Their meta-channel is a bit unclear. Maybe they're inviting you, or perhaps they're not. You reply that you've also been wanting to see that same exhibit. Now you're communicating that you're not sure if it's an invitation, but that you'd like to go. If they aren't crazy about you, they can start talking about Vermeer, and thus communicate that they don't want to go with you. You can continue to have a civil conversation and not feel insulted.

If you instead focus on the content channel and say, "Hmm... I'm not sure if you're inviting me or not, but I'd like to go," you put them in a very awkward position. This is the exact type of conversation that should happen over the meta-channel so that neither person is made to feel bad.

Once you are tuned into the meta-channel, you might feel as though you are in the matrix. Even when people don't intend to communicate on the meta-channel, you can infer their sub-communications. You understand not just the "what" of people are saying, but also the way, and you gain the power to have two complete conversations at the same time.

The first step to communicating on the meta-channel is to continually ask yourself why people are saying the things they say. Why did he choose that exact phrasing? Why didn't she say something else instead? Why share that information now? Come up with some ideas in your head, and check them later when you have more information. By making predictions and verifying their accuracy then, you'll begin to calibrate your brain. When a prediction was off its mark, take the time to analyze and think about it.

Once you understand meta-communication, you want to start shaping yours. What we say can be interpreted in many different ways, so you have to craft what you speak for the specific person you're with whom you're talking. Try to create a simulator in your brain where, as you consider what to say, you predict how the listener will react, and what meaning they'll assign to it.

Sometimes when I read a non-fiction book, I decided that no matter what, I'm going to at least make one change as a result. I hope for a big breakthrough, but even a small tip can make a book worth reading. If you were to decide to do that with this book, I'd recommend having that change be focused on communicating more through the meta-channel.

Emotion

A lot of conversing is taking the other person on an emotional journey. You think about where they are emotional, as well as where they want to be, and you use the emotional channel to guide them there or keep them there if they're going to stay in the same place.

For example, let's say you meet someone at a concert. They're excited and having fun, which precisely is why they are at the show, so they want to maintain that state. If you initiate a severe talk about business, you are grossly miscommunicating on the emotional channel. Even if they enjoy business and being serious, it's so inappropriate in this context that they'll retreat from the conversation.

On the other hand, you could probably talk about business in an excited tone, and they'd engage with the conversation. The exact context would dictate whether it would work or not, but it's clear that it's a lot better than trying to be serious.

Consider someone who had a bad day and is frustrated. They probably want to shift to being happy and calm. You can slowly lead them in that direction by making the conversation increasingly positive. Maybe you'd start by matching their tone and asking them questions about the day, and then slowly bring some optimism to the discussion.

On the other hand, if someone were upset because they had a death in the family, though, they probably don't want to be happy. It just feels wrong. Maybe they want to feel understood and supported. You could communicate those things emotionally by listening, asking questions, and offering to do things to help.

Not every conversation is spiked with emotion, but there's usually some emotion there. If it's boredom, you've got to change that as soon as you can. If you're getting to know someone, maybe you'd want to emotionally communicate a little bit of mystery about yourself as well as excitement about getting to know them. Be aware of the emotional tone of the conversation and think about the directions you could move that emotion.

Status

There is an invisible hierarchy in every group of people from two on up. If a decision had to be made, who would make it? If there were a crisis, to whom would people in the group turn to solve it? Who has to be more careful about what they say?

Humans are hierarchical creatures. We want to know where we stand, not for vanity, but to inform how we speak and act.

I could propose any combination of your friends, and you could probably sketch out a hierarchy. Maybe it would be flat, everyone being a peer, but more likely there would be a leader or two who get spoken to with just a tiny bit more deference and take more responsibility for the group. Whatever the hierarchy, everyone in the group would probably unconsciously agree to it and act and speak accordingly.

When you join another companion gathering, you need to comprehend the chain of importance. As a pariah, it's fundamental to keep up the concordance of the group, and not irritate it. If you know how the individuals identify with one another, that will be much simpler to do. Indeed, even one on one, status is essential. Understanding somebody's status is seeing how they see their place on the globe.

And, of course, you want to communicate your status. Some people will treat everyone with respect, but others only treat people with respect if they demand it. So your default outgoing communication on the status channel with someone new should usually be that you deserve respect and are worth getting to know.

A lot of statuses is communicated nonverbally with body language and eye contact. Direct eye contact conveys high status universally. Taking up a lot of space with your body also conveys high status.

Talking about how high status you are conveys low status. So does doing almost anything that is inappropriate in context. If you take up a lot of space where there's space to spare, you will appear to be high-status. If you take up a lot of space on a train where there are people who want to sit down, you look insecure and hard.

Vocal tone also communicates a lot about status. Someone who talks slightly louder than average and with clarity will appear to be more critical.

Instinctively reading status from the way people act and speak is consistent and accurate, which indicates that it's harsh to fake. If you feel like someone is high status, they probably are. If you think they're overreaching and are trying to convince you that they're high status, they probably are faking.
For this reason, it's dangerous to try to fake your status through body language and tonality. As you become more comfortable and confident, these aspects of communication will naturally change positively.

However, much of status is about what you will and won't accept from yourself and others. That can't be faked, but it can be changed. For example, many people will agree with higher status people as a blanket policy. Your boss says that he thinks the food at a restaurant is terrible, and you agree with him even though you think it's great. The "cool guy" at a party loves a song, and suddenly everyone likes it, too. This is a low-status behavior that invites disrespect.

Disagreeing with everything is even worse, but expressing your own opinion in a clear and appropriate way conveys that you can think for yourself, even in the presence of strong outside influence. You will be given respect for doing this.

Another primary changeable status indicator is whether you take responsibility or not. If you're at a restaurant and someone needs to speak to the waiter about moving some tables together, are you the one who does so? When a conversation is flagging, do you take the initiative and revive it? Ever-so-surprisingly, being a leader, indicates to others that you are, in fact, a leader.

Be aware of what others are communicating on the status channel, and avoid mannerisms or habits that accidentally convey lower status. In general, you should be communicating that you are a peer to people with whom you want to become friends. If you feel like someone is making an effort to appear higher status than you, it's sometimes worth taking action like speaking louder and taking up more space to place yourself a hair above them, only because they've indicated that status is important to them and that they respond to a higher status.

Shifting Attentional Focus

A group of scientists was able to establish that when some test subjects were instructed to lay their focus on the people they were having a conversation with rather than themselves, it was found that they felt 67 percent more confident than before. These findings, when adopted, can help someone to start building their social skills step by step. Meaning that when you find yourself in any social situation, you should always try to focus on the person you are talking to, rather than yourself.

If you keep on repeating the same action, you will come to notice how your mind shifts and starts focusing inwards thoughts such as "I'm now getting nervous" or "someone is thinking that I am awkward" and so on. While all these are common occurrences for someone who is trying to master social skills, it doesn't mean that you let those thoughts hinder your progress to becoming an all-around person. When it happens that way, you can save the situation by simply forcing yourself to start asking yourself questions regarding those around you instead. Questions such as "What are they working with?" "If she's an artist as she claims, what kind of art is that?" "How is he going to spend his free time?" and many more can considerably have a positive impact when it comes to shifting your attentional focus.

When your head is filled up with questions about others, it will take you a while to get used to those questions, but with enough practice, everything will happen automatically. Your brain will become less self-aware, making you more self-confident in the course of learning how to become socially endowed. Not only that. Also, you will have numerous questions lingering in your mind about how you can hold a constructive conversation with other people without necessarily losing your focus on attention.

Alternatively, you may move your conversation forward by asking those around you the questions that you already have in your mind. You can start by asking questions like, "You said, you are an artist, what type of an artist are you?" "Where do you come from?" "What do you specialize in?" among others to help you gain some little confidence as well as experience slowly by slowly.

Memorize a Few Questions

There are a set of questions that you can devote part of your free time to memorize. Such matters will play a very significant role when having a conversation with someone you are not familiar with. Additionally, those questions will instill some confidence in you given that you will always have something to fall back on during a conversation in any social setup. Having confidence is a critical factor that you will need to master if at all, you are looking forward to having your social skills top notch. This is the case, especially when you are faced with people that look intimidating to you. Portraying your social skills more confidently will set you way above everyone else in any social situation. It is good to understand the dynamics of a social world, and if you don't have the necessary skills, then you will not stand a chance to express yourself before other people.

Learn a Few Tricks from Self-Confident People

Human beings are the smartest animals in the universe, but everyone learns new concepts, ideas, skills and actions from others. That is why there are role models, those who inspire and motivate others, and those who are celebrated because of what they have in their lives. That being said, there is no better way of learning a new idea or concept if not from someone you consider to be unique.

Take a good example of confident people in the showbiz and learn how they behave. Perhaps you are a great fan of James Bond, George Clooney, Oprah Winfrey or even Cristiano Ronaldo. It is no doubt that you consume a good percentage of your free time thinking, fantasizing, wishing and dreaming of being like one of these confident people. And the most exciting part of this observation is that you cannot afford to miss watching their films, their talk shows, listening to their interviews and reading about them in various magazines. What doesn't hit you is the fact that they are confident people and you can be like them if you learn how they carry themselves.

In reality, you should not think of faking who you indeed are unless you want to get a rude shock of your life shortly. Pretending self-confidence in a social situation may work for you at certain times but not always. Therefore, spend a little of your time and learn a few tricks from your role models, influential people and your peers. Make sure you apply what you have learned from others in a more appropriate way that will not bring you out as a fake person. No one likes associating with fakes. What it means by learning a few tricks from self-confident people is to get an overall idea of how you can confidently express yourself in a social situation. This can be done verbally, assuming a new posture, creating eye-contact, changing facial expression and using all necessary social values to gain an advantage over others.

Starting gradually to acquire social skills entails a lot, and you should be ready to venture further afield if you want to be seen as a social person. Even though you may face some difficulties along the way, it doesn't mean that you despair and fall out before achieving your goals. You should know that it takes a great sacrifice for one to succeed, and you should be ready to do what it takes for you to improve on your social skills.

Chapter 4: Give Genuine Compliments

Who doesn't like being complimented? Of course, everyone loves positive compliments for their achievements, looks, style of dressing and actions. Compliments are part of our extraordinary components of social life. When done in the right manner, they can create a lot of positive energy among individuals making things happen as if by magic. Positive compliments ease the tension or atmosphere around two people as well as disposing people to each other.

But there is a better way of giving them and receiving them as well. And everyone, including you, needs to know the best way to do both. All you have to do is to get it done right, or your compliment might be taken the wrong way. But the key to giving genuine compliments lies in your ability to say something that you honestly think and believe to be true. After that, you can then deliver your compliments in a more sincere tone of your voice. Who knows, you might create an everlasting impression on someone. So, which is the right way to deliver genuine compliments as one step towards improving your social skills?

Just Keep Real

To make your compliment look real, find one thing that you genuinely like about that person you are praising. This should not be a problem for you, provided that you know how to do it right, to make the person feel good from your compliment. You can start by saying something like "Your shirt is nice. I like it" or "You have nice hair" and so on. Keep in mind that any compliment you make about someone goes more profound than you can imagine, and it should leave both of you feeling happy. To get it even better, take a while and study the person to find what you admire the most before proceeding with saying anything. However, your compliment will be positively made if it is clear that you mean what you say to the person.

On the other hand, don't take someone for granted by giving a false a compliment. This may not go down well if the person finds out that your praise is not genuine. For example, if you come across your friend wearing a new blouse or a pair of shoes you feel are tacky, don't go ahead and make a compliment. Doing so will have two possible outcomes; she will believe you or she will take it the other way thinking that your praise is some form of sarcasm. If that is your habit of making compliments that you don't mean, then you won't look sincere to your friend.

In the long run, your compliments will be taken for granted or brushed off by those you are fully aware of your habit.

Take advantage of someone's point of pride to give your genuine compliments. This will make someone feel more special even though it is clear that you first noticed something unique that matters most to that person you are talking to. For instance, if your next-door neighbor spends most of his time cultivating his beautiful flower garden, can give your compliment based on his excellent gardening skills and eye for color. Praising someone for what they are good at is one way of making them feel appreciated and motivated to keeping doing what they love most. Your compliments could change someone's life for better, if at all, they target a specific point of pride in that person.

Think of something that is not obvious when giving your compliments genuinely. This is an excellent tactic that needs you to pick out anything that isn't noticeable by many people when praising them. This shows that you should keep a keen eye on the person to the extent of noticing something unique. Such non-obvious compliments make a significant impact on many people, and they are likely to remember and cherish your good praises for many years to come. For instance, you can start by telling your colleague that you have noticed how hardworking she is and you have a feeling that she's somehow talented in what she does. Or rather, you could go ahead and tell the girl next door that you admire her elegance and sense of fashion and that she inspires many women, both young and old, in your neighborhood. If no other person has ever made such a compliment to her, you will stand to have an easy field-day when it comes to winning her heart. This is because your praise will stand out and make her feel special or appreciated by you.

When making compliments, ensure that you don't use the same words for everyone. If you go about telling people in your neighborhood, "Hi, I like your outfit" or anything that sounds similar to that, in the end, those you compliment won't feel that special. Just be a little bit creative when complimenting different people on their positive attributes and in return, everyone will feel appreciated by your little praises.

Lay your focus on achieving more than just physical traits. It feels good for someone to tell you, "You look pretty," or "I like your new outfit" but keep at the back of your mind that the best compliments for anyone are those that point out to someone's impressive personal qualities or significant achievements. They are praising people for what they have worked so hard to achieve means more than giving a person compliments on something that they haven't strived to accomplish. This could be something like the color of their eyes or the size of their hair. Excellent and genuine compliments on other people can significantly improve your social skills. Such praises will make it easier for you to initiate and sustain a conversation with people around you.

Generously complimenting someone should not be confused with excessively. A limit has to be reached so that the other person does not get bored or feel overpraised. In other words, showering someone with many compliments will make the whole thing look less meaningful and annoying to some extent. Therefore, make your praises sparingly and at the right time to make your words resonate even more. To achieve that, you must start by spreading your compliments out to various people. Giving praises to one person over and over could mean something else, and the person may wrongly take you to be somehow obsessed. Compliment only when it is necessary, or there is something worth bringing up. Don't do it for the sake of appearing relevant when, in the real sense, you are not creating any positive impact on the person you are showering with many compliments.

Express Yourself Sincerely

Make sure that you express your compliments warmly. When giving compliments in any social situation, what matters the most is the way you deliver everything to someone. But there is no perfect way of doing so if you do not sound sincere. This is to mean that you need to mean what you say and how you express yourself so that every time you praise someone, you are not taken wrongly. Let the person you are complimenting know that you are serious with what you are saying. You can do so by ensuring that the person gets your message directly and explicitly. Also, it is of great importance to read the situation around you before taking the next step to compliment someone. For instance, if your female workmate walks into the office wearing a blouse with some funny-looking patterns on it and everyone is looking, you should not make any compliment that might draw the attention of those around to her. It might seem like you are out there to embarrass her before your other colleagues.

While praising someone, express yourself sincerely through your smile but not laughing. A pleasant smile should accompany a kind and genuine compliment in a social set up or given with some seriousness and sincere expression. Laughing, in this case, might be misinterpreted. The person will not be able to tell if you are truly serious or just joking. And this can ruin the whole idea behind your compliment. Try to smile and not laugh while you are giving a tribute to someone unless the other person appreciates it with some humor.

Nothing assures the other person of your sincerity more than making an eye-contact when giving a compliment. This is an easy way that will tell the other person that you mean what you are saying. Making eye contact is one of the many forms of nonverbal means of communicating with people. This helps people to understand one another better. Avoiding eye-contact by looking down or looking away makes you appear insincere in comparison to keeping an eye-contact while having a dialogue with someone.

Your tone is equally important, and it makes a lot of differences when giving a compliment to someone. The tone of your voice can make the other person know how genuine you sound hence the need to do your best when expressing yourself as you mean it. Don't create a weird tone that will be misinterpreted in the wrong way. The best compliment is one which leaves no room for any misunderstandings.

When done right, your recipient will know that you are serious and mean every single word you say. At the end of the conversation, everyone will come out feeling good and satisfied with it. However, it may sound simple, but it is always common for compliments to have hidden meanings. For instance, when you seem a little sarcastic, it may send a wrong message to other people by making them think that you are making fun of them, which might not be true. Alternatively, some tones can make others feel you are jealous of the person you are extending your compliments to. Make sure you do it just right so that others will not take you in a wrong way. A sincere tone is an added advantage, especially when you are trying to socialize with others out there.

Some researches point out clearly that a show of kindness is contagious. In this context, paying someone with a genuine compliment will also make the same person do the same to someone else, and that chain of events might continue that way among different groups of people. But it is prudent to exactly know what to be avoided as far as paying compliments to others is concerned.

To begin with, you should always be on the lookout not to make serious mistakes of yelling at your friend or colleagues walking down the street because this is insulting and embarrassing. The whole concept of making a compliment is to make you and others feel good. Yelling or shouting around will not only make you look awkward in public but will make the other person feel uneasy. Well, for others, it may sound normal, but it all depends on the manner with which you are interactions with each other. If it is a stranger, the outcome could be something else.

On the other hand, you should be careful not to upset others by making demeaning comments. Such comments will not be taken in kind by others and can brand you more negatively. Find the appropriate way to make better comments by being respectful and polite. After all, there is only a straightforward way everyone receives a compliment, and this is when it is done graciously with a genuine smile. Receiving a tribute teaches everyone critical lessons about life. Key among them is how they feel highly subjective to others, and that feeling is only known to them. This is because each given compliment creates a positive atmosphere that is powerful enough to have an everlasting impression in everyone's heart.

Compliments make the better part of everyday conversation, and they can play a very significant role in shaping your social skills. That is why you should know how to express yourself when complimenting someone and also see the kind of impact you are creating between you and the other party. If done with the right attitude, tone, respect, and politeness, nothing will stand your way from being a social person.

Making Eye Contact

Short and sweet-- always make eye contact. In every conversation you have, you should maintain eye contact eighty percent of the time or more. Studies show that, while controlling for other variables, eye contact causes people to like and trust each other more.

Eye contact indicates that the person you're speaking with has your full attention and is important to you. If those two things aren't right, it's probably better not to have the conversation in the first place. Not making eye contact is dismissive and rude. Look away to think or pause, but when you are speaking, or the other person is speaking, you should look into their eyes.

You probably already do this so that I won't belabor the point. But I've met people who make almost no eye contact, and it's incredibly uncomfortable talking with them.

Be Easily Distracted During Your Own Stories

There's nothing better than hearing a great story, and almost nothing worse than being stuck listening to a bad story that won't end. For that reason, you want to make sure that your stories last a long time if the other person is really into them and are cut short if they aren't interested.

The easiest way to do this is to be easily distracted whenever you're telling a story, even if you think it's the best story you have.

If you can find a way to stop talking, maybe because someone has interrupted your conversation or because the waiter has brought your food, take that opportunity and never deliver the story back up. Just assume that it's dead. If your friend interrupts you, switch to whatever they're talking about.

If the other person is interested, they will bring the topic back up. No one is too shy to ask to hear the rest of a fascinating story. And if they're not interested, the story dies. That's frustrating sometimes because it's fun to tell stories, but telling someone a story they aren't interested in hearing is always negative.

As you do this, pay attention to which stories never get brought back from the dead, and bias your-self towards not telling them to other people. Some stories are good, some are duds, and certain people will only enjoy some. It's good to know which is which.

The better you know someone, the less you have to drop your stories. Eventually, you know people well enough to make intelligent predictions about which stories they'll enjoy and which they won't. So most stories you'll tell the whole way through. If you detect even a whiff of disinterest, you can drop the story gracefully.

On the other hand, always allow others to finish their stories, even if they're boring. You can break this rule for very close friends who appreciate blunt criticism, but that will be a tiny minority of the people with whom you interact.

Your goals in a conversation are to make sure that the other person enjoys themselves, to allow them to learn about you, and for you to learn about them. By allowing them to tell a story that's not all that interesting, you are letting them enjoy themselves, and you're also learning about them, even if it's in a tedious format.

Crossing the Line

In any given social situation, there's a bounding line that dictates what's polite and what's too intimate. This line is defined by the relationship between the people in the conversation. For example, you could tell your best friend that he's gaining weight and should hit the gym, but you would never say that to a stranger.

Another example is the tone and texture of the language used. With a new contact in a professional setting, profanity, certain colloquialisms, or slang would be outside the line.
Some people routinely cross this line, but they are very few. Usually, the breaches are along the lines of slang or profanity, rather than genuinely offending someone. On the other hand, I'd contend that the vast majority of people draw the line too tightly.

Friendships deepen with voluntary increases in intimacy. There's a wag the dog sort of effect where deepening associations cause affection to increase, but it also works in reverse.

When two people begin communicating, both are, among other things, trying not to look foolish. Safe opinions and pleasantries never make someone look like a fool, so very often they are the topics that people stick to when they aren't well acquainted.

Chapter 5: Pay Attention to Your Body Language

It may take you by surprise to learn that your body language contributes the most when communicating with others. Sounds strange, uh?! According to the research, your actual words constitute well up to 7 percent of what you correctly convey, your tone of voice takes up 38 percent, and your body language takes the lion's share of a whopping 55 percent. This is awesome, and it shows how unconscious human beings are when communicating among themselves. That is the main reason you need to pay particular attention to your body language as a nonverbal form of communication to improve your social skills.

Steps to Help You Achieve that Confident Body Language

Before we get to the heart of the matter, you should ask yourself some simple questions as regards to your social life. Questions such "Are you a social over thinker?" can help you find answers to your current social standings and from there you will be in a better position to start improving your conversation skills, ability to bond with others and your confidence.

However, the following steps will help you achieve that confident body language to change your social life forever:

Always maintain a confident appearance

Have you come across this common phrase that goes, "Look good, feel good"? Well, it is just a simple, but catchy Instagram hashtag used today. It means that when you devote some of your time to take care of your whole body and appearance, in the long run, you will start feeling good about yourself for obvious reasons: you will look happier, healthier and proud of your new look. Consequently, it will have a positive impact on your body language in general. You will soon discover that you are more confident than before, and those around you will start treating you differently.

Most significantly, your hygiene will take center stage in transforming that part of you responsible for making you look competent and confident at the same time. As the saying goes, "cleanliness is next to godliness," and in this case, let your cleanliness be next to your confidence. And you can achieve this goal in a simple way that will contribute mainly to being a well-groomed person from the toes to the head. Taking showers and brushing your teeth regularly, dressing in clean clothes and taking good care of your hair is but a few examples of what it takes to look at part and parcel of a decent person. Sadly a good percentage of people overlook this fact without knowing the impact it can create to others. Looking clean will give you confidence and help you eliminate that uncomfortable feeling of being untidy. On top of that, dressing in clothes that are appropriate for the season or an event turns out to be yet another easy way of feeling and appearing confident before other people at a given social setup.

Adopt a confident posture

Looking clean and well-dressed is not all that is necessary to make you look that confident. There is more than meets the eye when it comes to a nonverbal form of communication that is likely to have a positive impact on your social skills. This is a very significant step that needs you to hold your body in a manner that will bring out the aspect of confidence in you. As a result, your confident posture will make you stand way above everyone else.

What comes in your mind when you think of adopting a confident posture? Most of the people would expect something that has been passed down in every generation starting from the medieval kings and queens to the current generation. Yes, this might sound like a posture depicting the ramrod-straight back with arms held out your sides or instead of a sort of some hard position that makes you appear very upright. Contrary to your expectations, that is not what it means to have a confident posture.

Alternatively, slouching, crossing your arms, and keeping your head down are body postures that will make you look smaller, petrified and full of insecurity. Under no circumstance should you think of putting yourself in such an awkward position which is likely to make other people misjudge you?

So, what is left to describe a confident posture clearly? The correct description of a confident stance comes in between the above explanations. It is true that you are supposed to stand upright, but that doesn't imply that you hold uncomfortably straight. In other words, if the way you hold feels unnatural to you, then it probably appears strange too.

The second instance that can make you look confidence is keeping your chin up. Don't confuse this with sticking your chin out in the air or tucked away into your collar bone. At the same time, try as much as possible to have your hands loosely by your sides and make sure that either hand is casually tucked inside your pocket or make natural hand gestures when giving a speech.

How you hold your body tells a lot about yourself and how you feel. Depending on where you are or your target audience, your body language can send mixed reactions to different people. However, making some minor adjustments can significantly cause you to look more confident and well composed when having a conversation.

Make sure your hands and feet are confident

Your hands and feet are far more critical parts of your body. You can imagine how life would be without them. As such, your hands and feet can influence how others perceive you. These body parts are known to send great messages about your state of self-esteem. Your hands and feet give an accurate picture of what you are thinking and what you are about to do or say.

No wonder it is no longer a mystery when you hear a policeman asking you to keep your hands where they can be seen. Since your hands are quite capable of anything, seeing them gives the police officer some amount of assurance that you are not holding anything that can compromise anyone's safety. But when your hands are not fully visible, it may suddenly brand you a threat to others, and the police might take drastic measures to neutralize the situation in a bid to protect others and himself as well. Anyway, this doesn't just apply to law enforcement, but rather it is a universal human instinct to have complete trust if someone's hands are visible. And if you are keen enough, you will notice that people do it consciously in situations that bring them out as being harmless. Perhaps that could be the main reason at some point you offered your hand to be sniffed by a dog that is unfamiliar with you. Or better still, that is why you are likely to end up holding your hands out when you are pleading with someone.

Alternatively, keeping hands free and visible is a component of a confident body language which you should adopt when in a social situation.

Apart from that, you might come across some people who wittingly resort to picking at their fingernails, mess their hair or even fiddle with their outfits or accessories whenever they get nervous. In most cases, such people may not be aware of what they are doing, but other people will. If that happens to you, keep in mind that your insecurity will be transparent to those close to you at that moment.

Your walking style is another giveaway as far as your body language is concerned. The way you walk can tell a lot about your confidence. If you walk while taking teeny-tiny steps, shuffling your feet or misbehaving by tip-toeing, it will make people think that you're suspicious, scared or frighteningly strange. All these are not desirable outcomes when it comes to interacting with others.

But taking longer strides as well as keeping your eyes fixed on where you are heading to is a clear indication that you are confident in what you are doing. This is a perfect explanation of walking purposely with enough confidence.

And now the stance that you assume immediately after walking is also a significant contributor to your general appearance of confidence. Your position alone does not convince anyone of your confidence. For example, taking a narrow stance could make you appear smaller just in the same way as tucking your chin or hunching your shoulders.

How you stand plays a critical role in determining how confident you are. Standing while taking up extra space than usual with your feet shoulder width apart, is a good indication that you're optimistic. The same is true when you sit with both feet planted firmly on the floor to show that you are confident as well. The two instances show that you are sure of where you belong and that you are not afraid of what you are doing. Maintaining a comfortable stance while taking up a substantial amount of space for your entire body size makes you look and feel more confident than standing as if you are on an overly full elevator.

Your eyes too should be confident

Your eyes act as a portal to your mind. Many times, people's intentions could be read right from their eyes, and this makes this vital sense of sight organs the fourth and the last component of developing a confident body language with the sole purpose of improving your social skills. Staying down at the ground, looking at your hands away from the person you are speaking to indicates that you are either guilty or are shy, insure and terrified. In short, your eye contact is key to being confident.

Unlike all other concepts, this one is simple and straightforward. It doesn't require a formula or some specialized training, but it only encourages you not to be afraid to look at other people when speaking with them. Being afraid of looking back at people means that you probably don't want them to look at you either. And this is one sign of insecurity in many people who are not confident about themselves.

So, should you find yourself in a situation that requires you to put on a little bit of your confident body language, think of your general appearance, posture, hands feet, and your eyes? Just know that a picture is worth a thousand words, and what people see in you by looking at you is worth a million words. Therefore, make it count.

Best Ways to Convey Some Confidence Through Your Body Language

Have you ever heard of some people saying, "Fake it till you make it?" This is a common phrase that is used for different reasons and circumstances. More often than not, you will be shocked to realize that nine times out of 10, the phrase is used to refer to a common habit of faking confidence.

Although faking is not an acceptable thing in different societies across the globe, the amount of confidence that people exude play a critical role in what they usually experience throughout their personal lives, social lives and at the workplace. Even though you may not feel confident enough to face any situation, but the ability to act confident can become a valuable skill to your advantage.

It doesn't mean you get to the podium at a given gathering and surprise your audience by telling them how confident you are on that particular day. What it means is that you need to act like you are a confident person even if you not to let others judge you by themselves. It doesn't look right to blow your own trumpet in public; you might look utterly irrelevant or create a fool out of your sudden excitement. It seems better when you exude your confidence through your body language rather than verbally. This way, it portrays a clear and genuine picture of who you are, and others might judge you in a good move based on your actions.

Body language has been known to be the best form of nonverbal communication because it brings out your thoughts and attitude. It doesn't matter whether you have to be aware of it or not, but what is important to know is that your body language is continuously sending a message that is read by your immediate audience. And your body language does not need someone special to decipher its true meaning.

Some of the practical examples of our body language are indeed the everyday things we see all the time. These may constitute seeing someone standing with the head tilted back, arms crossed, eyes pointed to the ceiling, shifting the body weight back and forth and tapping one foot on the ground. When you notice someone in this situation, what should come in your mind is that the person is either frustrated or impatient.

But in a situation where someone is sprawled out on a chair with the arms above the head and one leg right up on the table, it is obvious this particular individual is in a comfort zone. People in a similar situation don't need to explain to you how they are feeling. It is obvious to make out how they are doing by merely reading their body language. This is a vital thing to keep at the back of your mind when applying your social skills.

Keep making an eye-contact as much as you can

Inability to make eye-contact is a tale-tell sign of your insecurity. When you avoid looking straight in someone's eyes during a conversation shows that you are comfortable, shy or you are probably trying to hide something.

On the other hand, it doesn't send a positive message to other people when you make a creepy eye-contact. This is a sign of sincerity and confidence in you when you consistently meet the other person's eyes when in a conversation, you will look genuine and interested in what both of you are discussing. Making eye contact frequently is not enough, but you need to maintain a constant blinking pattern to stop distracting the other person or sending a completely wrong message. In case your conversation involves many people, ensure that you switch making your eye-contact from one person to the other rather than focusing on a particular person. Generally speaking, eye contact is one of the most important indicators of a confident body language.

Maintaining proper posture

Look at the most confident people around you and try to find out how they always position themselves in a social setup. You will realize a common trend in most if not all. Confident people are known to stand up straight and hold their heads up high in readiness to face anything coming their way. A good posture regarding confidence does imply that it has to be stiff as many people think. It should be a relaxed one that allows plenty of movement.

Keeping your head down, hunching over, crossing your arms or folding into yourself, portray signs of shame, fear, and insecurity. Pay particular attention to the way you conduct yourself when you are nervous and then make an effort to compose yourself by generally standing in such a situation instead. If you are not sure about yourself, you can talk to your friends or family members to give you a clear picture of your behavior looks like when you are nervous or uncomfortable. This will help you be more aware of yourself in the future, and you can always work hard to overcome such feelings whenever you are in an uncomfortable situation.

Make some movements

Apart from portraying a relaxed and open posture, those who are known to be confident are also comfortable moving around a lot. Before you get it wrong, ensure that you draw a line between fidgeting and walking around. Also, you will need to put into consideration other signs that show your nervousness such as pacing, twisting your earring, fiddling with your buttons on the shirt, messing with your hair among others as clear indicators of lacking confidence. Other signs that can betray your confidence include stiffness as a result of keeping hands clenched in fists or deep into your pockets to indicate some discomfort. On the contrary to all that, confident body language involves hand gestures, facial expressions and any other form of natural movement that is appropriate for that particular situation.

Facial expressions

Many people find it difficult to control their facial expressions as one of the aspects of body language. Through such expressions, one can quickly reveal how you are feeling and what you are thinking about from the feelings you make on your face. But with experience, you will undoubtedly be in a better position to maintain your facial expressions more confidently despite the situation at hand.

Keep in mind that confident people smile a lot because they believe in their ability to handle all situations coming their way. At the same time, those people lack the insecurity, thus allowing them to have full control of themselves.

Have you ever known that when you are nervous, you don't smile a lot? By now, you know it. Therefore, make sure that you laugh when it is appropriate to do so to look bold and confident. In addition to that, you should avoid pursuing your lips, biting your lips, clenching your jaw and blinking unnaturally or rapidly. Just think of what makes you nervous when socializing with others so you may find a way to focus on maintaining an excellent facial expression that will bring an aspect of confidence in you.

Your body language is a universal language that should be nurtured even more so that you may use it to your advantage when socializing with other people. Numerous things bring out the aspect of your body language, and the more you discover them, the better you become when expressing yourself. Have full control of your body language and work towards improving your social skills.

Chapter 6: Stay Abreast of the Current Affairs

For you to be a social person, there is a need to have outstanding conversational skills, among other things. The ability to hold a good conversation with one or more people lies in your knowledge of different topics that you can comfortably express yourself right in front of other people. That is why you have to find a way of sustaining almost any conversation by contributing to what others are discussing to improve your social skills. And there is no better way of doing so if not staying abreast with the current affairs in the form of news, the latest piece of technology on the market, history, politics, sports, romance, literature, show-biz and the common gossip in your city and beyond.

However, you don't have to master every topic that comes your, but you may choose a few niches where you think you are comfortable with nearly everything. But it is essential to know the source of your knowledge and verify if it is reliable.

With numerous social media platforms emerging each day, it is becoming increasingly difficult to tell the difference between real news and fake ones, and if you are not careful enough, you can quickly get swept away with sources that peddle lies and propaganda. So, how do you manage to stay abreast with the current affairs, and how do you apply that knowledge to your social skills? Let's find out.

Staying Abreast of News

At the moment you can obtain news-both national and international-from various sources. These are social media platforms, mobile applications, notifications, from your friends and of course, traditional radio and TV stations, among others. With the increase of internet use, partisan and opinionated news is becoming a familiar source of news lately compared to a few decades back.

This new trend has been witnessed whereby most of the media consumers tend to shift their attention from the traditional news outlets of the all-time objective journalism to other emerging sources. The fact that the opinion-oriented sources of news are entertaining, it doesn't mean that they are reliable sources of news. Such references are likely to exaggerate or slant the stories which (unfortunately) may not be apparent. For that reason and many others, it is prudent that you find just a few trusted traditional sources of news if at all you want to receive accurate and substantiated news.

It will look awkward to use false information and eventually mislead others. In the end, the backlash from those you were innocently misleading could have some repercussions on your social skills, and that is not what you want to experience. In other words, you may be branded a liar, and it will take a substantial amount of time and effort to make others have trust in you again. Therefore, you might consider listening to news from a few reliable traditional news sources such as the British Broadcasting Corporation (BBC), Cable News Network (CNN), Al Jazeera, Fox News, CNBC, National Public Radio (NPR) and the New York Times among others.

Listening to news podcasts is another excellent way of sourcing information. Most of the news podcasts make a summary of the daily events in about 15 to 30 minutes segments. These news podcasts will keep you on the edge of your seat with all important news highlights of the day, especially if you are always short on time to sit down and follow news from the traditional sources. Subscribe to news podcasts to stay well-informed on the current events without necessarily spending much of your time searching for news. Some of the best examples of news podcasts are the BBC Business Daily: Behind the Stats or The New Yorker: Comments and 5 Live Hit List and many more.

With the spread of the internet, you may take advantage of this form of communication by subscribing to Google Alerts. This is a customized notification service that will allow you to set several alerts with Google on any topic of your interest. Every time the issue pops up on the internet, you will automatically receive notifications from Google.

For your convenience, Google allows well up to 1,000 topics for each email address. In this way, you have the option of setting alerts from a broader spectrum of subjects. What you need to do is merely going to https://www.google.com/alerts/ and proceed by entering the terms with which you want to get notifications for. This website allows you to select the types of news sources of your interest, the frequency which you wish to get the alerts and finally, the email address through which you will get alerted whenever those topics you selected pop up on the web.

For instance, you may want to set up Google Alerts from a specific region, city or subject so that anytime information touching on what you have chosen comes up; you will immediately get notified through an email address. Likewise, you can set alerts for specific people of your interest, such as a president, a celebrity, or even your favorite sportsman. Anytime these people are mentioned on the website; you will be sure of reading about them through the notification received in your email address.

In a standard setup, you will agree that most of the discussions among different groups of people revolve around some iconic figures in society, politics, sports, and celebrities. To blend in seamlessly with those around you, you will have to contribute to their discussion. That is why it is essential to have some background information on the topic of discussion.

Are you aware of the news aggregators? If not, then it is essential to have an idea about them. News aggregators are a great source of information whereby they pull similar stories from various news sources and then group them according to their respective subjects. These stories are delivered to you in the form of an email list, and they have been proven to be a great way to help you stay abreast of current affairs and news in general. Most significantly, news aggregators source information from a variety of sources and compile all of them in one place.

How does it work? A news aggregator searches some news sources by picking out all articles on a specific topic and then arrange them in an accessible and digestible format for you. You can check for any matter of your interest from news aggregators like Flipboard, Google Current, and Taptu by downloading their mobile app on your device. This is a convenient way of sourcing information hassle free.

Keeping up with Local News

There are numerous ways to keep up with local news, and some of the common ones are through subscribing to a local paper, watching your local broadcast television, using the radio for updates and news coverage, signing up for news summaries, paying attention to social media and reading from blog posts.

Newspapers have been there since time immemorial, and their popularity as a great source of information doesn't seem to go down any time soon. As time passes, many papers keep on relying on and trusting local newspapers when it comes to sourcing for the latest news. The papers cover a wide range of subjects touching on social events, crime, education, sports, business news, and local government. Also, they include a broader topical area in comparison to other local sources of news. Their influence on the masses comes about as a result of being in the category of those news sources with in-depth coverage of different topics. In these papers, you will not fail to stumble on local politics, investigative reports, and more detailed information on current affairs. This means that you can become highly knowledgeable on almost any topic through local papers given that they cover nearly all subjects in greater depth.

Unlike local newspapers, local broadcast television covers a few events but in greater depth with more exposure. Local broadcast television stations are part of the most significant percentage of the local media in various cities, and it is no surprise that they are among the most trusted sources of vital information on some sensitive topics.

Radios have been in use for quite a long time, and they are still popular despite the ever-evolving world of technology. Many people regard frequency Modulated (FM) radio as the best source of news and information on local issues. Local radio stations are a rich source of information covering some topics from accidents, traffic jams, collisions, morning news reports, investigative reporting, talk shows, and many others. You can use that information to enrich yourself with enough knowledge that can help you stay abreast of the current affairs. This is helpful in one way or the other when it comes to engaging friends in a conversation.

Better still, you can make good use of your mobile devices to access relevant information by signing up for news summaries. A section of news sources is now providing daily, and weekly reviews are highlighting current affairs. To have access to news summaries, what you can do is signing up to receive these condensed stories via your email inbox.

In the world where social media rules every sphere of influence, you can never claim to miss out on any story, whether it's fake or real. These platforms are quite entertaining and bringing people together virtually. And in this century you will look out of place if you are not a member of any of those social media websites. From Facebook to Twitter and WhatsApp to Telegram and others, no single hour passes without a new story coming up.

Facebook, for instance, is the mother of all social media platforms and millions upon millions of pages are available to bring together like-minded individuals. You can start by liking your government agencies and local media outlets on Facebook or following your favorite media personalities on Twitter so that any time there is something new coming up; you will get notifications and react immediately.

Currently millions are accessing these platforms, and whenever a clip of sensitive news is uploaded, it takes a matter of minutes to go viral. This means news spread fast on social media when users share on their walls for others to see. This chain reaction has made social media to become the best place to source or share information. However, on the social point of view, you can learn a lot of skills that can help to improve your social skills in the real world.

From social media, we now shift our attention to blogs. These are internet-based media that takes up most of the entire media landscapes by focusing on local or international issues. There are many bloggers, and each of them specializes in different areas when discussing local issues. The internet is full of blog posts that talk substantively on issues affecting different people and places. Even though bloggers have come on the spotlight to tackle the critical problems in society, it doesn't mean that everything they write about is right. Others are paid to propagate fake news, and if you are not keen enough, you may find yourself caught between real and fake news. This is not to discourage you from reading blogs, but it is a piece of advice to make you aware of the prevailing situation in the world where news comes from various sources without being verified.

Staying abreast about current affairs is one of the most important ways to improve your social skills. Every time you come across something new, know that you are enriching your general knowledge, which in turn plays a crucial role in your social life. It is evident that when people come together, they talk among themselves and their topic of discussion varies from group to group or person to person thus the need to be fully known to seize the occasion in your favor. If you are abreast with what is going on around you and in other parts of the world, you can use that knowledge to spice up your game when it comes to initiating and sustaining a meaningful conversation with different people. This way, your social skills will become better and better as you access information on current events from various sources.

Chapter 7: Overcome Your Negative Thoughts

Negative thoughts can harm your social behavior by shutting you off from the rest of the world. There is a common belief that our minds control our bodies and how we relate to our surrounding. So you can imagine how much damage you can cause to yourself by only letting your negative thoughts to control everything you do. Since no man is an island, you will find it near impossible to exist without allowing other people into your life.

If you find yourself in a situation where you experience a harsh inner critic, stress, anxiety, depression, worried or struggling with depression, chances are you are struggling with your negative thoughts. All these are clear signs that you are not doing well, and an immediate solution needs to be found as soon as possible.

This kind of thoughts can be detrimental to your well-being and have a devastating impact on your relationship, work, health and life in general. Worse of the worst, your social life will take an entirely new course, which might not be of any importance to you.

However, you can always find your way out of this predicament and eventually lead a more fulfilling life. A life where you will freely express yourself and interact with anyone you come across. But one question that is probably lingering in your mind now is how to overcome your negative thoughts in a bid to improve your social skills. Here are a few steps that will help you regain your self-worth so you may live happily just like other social people.

Recognize and Stay Clear of Negative Thought Patterns

Negative thought patterns keep recurring from time to time, and they are regarded as unhelpful thoughts. Such thoughts can lead to what is commonly described as negative, unpleasant, or unwanted emotions like depression, anxiety, stress, unworthiness, fear, shame, and so on.

Once you get to recognize and establish negative thought patterns when they occur, you can start to find ways to step back from them. This process (of stepping back from negative thoughts) is referred to as cognitive diffusion. During the process of cognitive diffusion, you are likely to visualize the thoughts in your head just as they are-thoughts and not anything tangible or in reality. This is because whenever you get fused with your thoughts (call it cognitive fusion), you tend to take your dreams with a lot of seriousness. With time you may start believing in them, buying into them, obeying them and playing with them as well.

On the other hand, you may not get fused in your thoughts or step back into cognitive defusion, and it can be concluded that you are not taking back your ideas very seriously. Instead, you are holding onto them lightly, and you only listen to them if you discover that they are more valuable than what you had previously thought.

In most cases, you don't take your thoughts to be 'the truth,' and you don't automatically come to obey them or play them out. With time, you will start seeing your thoughts as simply small bits of a language passing through your mind. These are mental events that move through your account every time you have negative thoughts.

Once you identify negative thought patterns within yourself, you can start thinking of the best way to get rid of them. Doing so will help you overcome negative thoughts while relieving you of the heavy burden of all attributes that come hand in hand with such views. In the end, you may feel relaxed, happier, and more open to accommodating new ideas, events, and people. Eventually, you may be able to walk out there with your head held high and make friends with a couple of people to test your social skills.

Identify Your Targets

Start by working out on those areas of your life that contribute more to your negative thoughts. These areas could be work-related issues or a bad relationship, which might affect your emotions leading to developing negative opinions about any situation you encounter. Therefore, you may make a list or keep an updated account of all your negative thoughts for a certain period. Then try your best to change how you think about one of those things that generally lead you into negative thoughts. But never approach them all at once unless you want to get more and more frustrated.

Every time you come to think about it, you should spare a little of your time asking yourself if at all, your thoughts are negative or positive. In case you find out that they are negative (which most likely is), challenge them and come up with ways to change their disposition into something positive.

For example, if you are being convinced that your boss thinks you are not performing at work-even when your work is outstanding-give yourself some motivation by reminding yourself that you are doing a great a job in the best way that you possibly can and that you will not allow anybody to undermine your effort by unfair criticism.

Once you feel that one area of your thinking has become more positive, move on to the next stage and repeat the same until you get everything right. However, overcoming negative thinking is not as easy as you might have thought. It takes time and your effort to start seeing good results. If you are not strong enough, you might give up along the way and remain in a perpetual state of self-denial.

Positive thoughts are suitable not only for your overall wellbeing but for your social life as well. Positive thinking cultivates a positive attitude inside you. And when you have a positive attitude, you will always treat every situation positively, and you will find getting along with others to be a straightforward task.

It doesn't mean that you have to think all the time positively. Negative thoughts are also part of your life. Life would be boring if everything comes our way so quickly. That is why challenges are there to shape our thinking while trying frantically to find a permanent solution to every situation. In other words, negatively thinking plays an equally important role in developing the way we live, talk, and socialize with others. But if you are looking to improve your social skills, it is time you change your negative thoughts into something more positive.

Don't Generalize

It is a common thing for negative thinkers to generalize almost everything. For instance, when you make a single mistake next to those people with negative thoughts, they will conclude that your job is outrightly wrong. Everything looks bad, smells and feels terrible in front of someone who is harboring some negative feelings.

On the other side, positive thinkers are more opened minded, happier and outgoing than negative thinkers. Positive thinkers try their best to avoid any negativity in their social life. They are always optimistic, friendly, accommodative, sociable, and willing to help where necessary. Just like anyone else, they still make mistakes in every aspect of their lives just in the same way as those who think negatively. The only difference here is how the two groups of individuals handle situations. Positive thinkers will wholeheartedly take full responsibility for their shortcomings, but the opposite is exact for negative thinkers.

Avoiding to generalize everything plays a role in changing someone's perspective. If you are a negative thinker, you can gradually change from seeing everything around you to be on the wrong side and try to accommodate everyone as they are. No two people are the same, and no two situations are the same, either. This means that you should think of not generalizing everything so that you can change your attitude and get accepted by everyone around you.

Start Interacting with Positive People

"Birds of the same feathers flock together." This is a common adage that can help you change from thinking negatively to thinking positively.   But it will all depend on your choice of those people you are going to spend your time with.

If those you are going to hang out with are negative thinkers, then it is apparent that you will behave and think like them. The same is true when you choose to spend your free time with positive thinkers. You will eventually adopt their way of life, how they speak, and how they relate to different people. Human beings are great learners, and you too, will also learn new vices from others. If possible take a while and join a group of positive thinkers to change your mindset.

This is not always easy as it may sound. Every human being is wired differently, and that is why we react differently when we meet new people, discover new ideas or go to a different place. It will not take you long to know that very few people choose who they want to associate with based on their tastes and preferences. For you to improve on your social skills, you will have no choice but to discard your group of negative thinkers so you may ally with positive thinkers. In the end, you will stand to benefit a great deal when it comes to displaying your social skills in different social situations.

Focus on Important Friendships

For most of my life, deciding how to spend my time wasn't much of a struggle. I had a few close friends, wasn't outgoing enough to make more, and had a lot of free time. So if someone wanted to hang out, I'd probably be able to join them without much thought. But then, a few years ago, that changed.

I had become consumed with my work. I'd stay home all day, sitting in front of the computer, chipping away at the work that lay before me. I loved being productive. But all of a sudden, I didn't have very much social time. I struggled to see all of my friends and realized that I didn't have the time to spend enough quality time with them.

So I decided that I would stop hanging out with everyone except for my closest friends and new friends that I was interested in becoming better friends with. I started saying no to most social invitations, including those with good friends where I felt it wouldn't be quality time. So I'd have tea with a good friend but wouldn't go to a birthday party of a friend's friend.

I never really thought about what the effects of this would be. It wasn't a calculated choice-- it was just a quick reaction to feeling like I was neglecting my best friends.

What happened, though, was remarkable. I didn't miss any of the social events I was now skipping. I'd feel a slight fear of missing out when I declined, but then when it was over, I was always pleased with how I used my time instead. But I expected that.

The surprise was what happened with existing friendships. By focusing all of my social time on my favorite people, my relationships with them improved. And the new friends who I kept seeing be-came better and better friends quickly.

The focus is such a powerful tool in learning and work, but we underestimate its benefit socially. By focusing my limited time on the people that matter most to me, those friendships become and stay very strong. And my social time is better than ever because all of it is with my favorite people or new people. I'm excited to get to know.

It can be scary and counterintuitive, when trying to improve your social skills, to say no to invitations or to trim down your roster of friends, but the focus makes it worth it. The goal isn't to have a million friends; it's to have a close group of amazing friends.

Different Types of Friendships

While it's always a good thing to have a local friend group that you cultivate and build, that doesn't mean that that's the only type of friendship worth having or putting effort into. In particular, you can have intense and satisfying friendships, even if you don't see the other person very often. You'd prefer to have the best people live right near you and be able to hang out in person whenever you're available, but that's not always possible. The "right person" part is the critical part, though, and it's worth investing in people even if the logistics aren't excellent.

For example, I have some friends in Austin who I love to death but only get to see once or twice per year. We don't talk much on the phone or online when I'm not there, but as soon as I land in Austin, it's like I never left. Sure, I'd instead that they live near me and travel with me a lot, but even though they don't, they're still close and valued friends.

I have a lot of friends who travel so much that we're always in flux. They'll come to visit Las Vegas, but I won't be home, and then I'll be in New York, and they're off traveling somewhere else. But every year or so we happen to be in some random country at the same time, and we get to reconnect.

Some friendships will be based on lots of time together, others on lots of conversations on the phone, and some just based on a few intense episodes together over the years.

You never know when people, including yourself, will move. Life is unpredictable for all of us. So even if you meet someone while traveling and don't know if or when you'll ever see them again, it's worth pursuing the friendship. Do that enough times, and you'll have the odds on your side for serendipitously reconnecting with them in the future.

On Not Being Intimidated

Sometimes you'll meet someone, or be trying to meet someone, which is intimidating. They seem so accomplished and funny and smart that you begin to question whether what you have to offer stacks up at all with what they have to offer.

There are two conventional approaches to this problem, neither of which works very well.

The first is to **come in low**. You act like a fan, ask a ton of questions to get a dialogue going, and then wait for an invitation of some sort. By doing this, you communicate low value and push the other person away. He'll be polite to you but will almost immediately rule out friendship. Not feeling like you have enough to offer becomes a self-fulfilling prophecy.

The second way is to **come in high**. You don't acknowledge the other person's accomplishments, and you compensate for your perceived lack of status by trying to impress. This always rings hollow, makes you seem inauthentic, and will also push the other person away.

So what can you do?

The first thing to realize is that you have to bring one thing, plus good social skills, to the table for someone to be interested in being your friend. Excellent social skills ensure that you don't impose on the other person, and one primary positive source of value is enough to make someone want to be your friend. Even the most sought after people like to have someone around who's funny, or tells good stories, or organizes cool events.

And no one is as good as their image suggests. Everyone has their weaknesses and insecurities. So even if someone seems like they're perfect, you can safely assume that they're not. They're probably an impressive person with a lot going for them, but no one is better than you in every way. You always have something to offer.

Treat everyone as equal, not because they are, but because they can be. People will often take on roles foisted upon them in social situations, and everyone is used to having peers around. If you act like a peer, you will usually be treated like one.

So it is easiest to create friendships with family members, and often more rewarding than other types of associations. If you have trouble making friends or are looking for a comfortable place to practice your social skills, start with your family. They're rooting for you already and will be a part of your life as long as anyone will be.

Focus on Friends and Eliminate Acquaintances

To simplify, let's say that there are three groups into which you could slot people you know. On the outside are acquaintances, next are friends, and in the center are close friends.

Acquaintances could be defined as people you'd only hang out with one-on-one if it were extremely convenient. Most of your interactions are probably in group settings, you end up having a one-on-one conversation by accident, and you'd never invite the other to something alone.

Friends are people you hang out with when convenient, maybe through shared interests. You don't connect on a deep emotional level, but perhaps you enjoy playing tennis together. You'll have meals together sometimes, but you wouldn't change your plans for them.

Close friends are the people you love. They're the people for whom you'd act against your best interests if the benefit to them were significant. They're the people whose success feels almost as good as your own, and with whom you can spend practically any length of time.

The value you exchange with an acquaintance is minimal. Your limited power to benefit them is on par with their limited ability to help you.

On the other end of the scale are close friends. The value exchanged between two close friends is enormous. Many studies show that people with more intimate ties to others live longer. There are a few significant factors that will define who you are, and close friendships are one of the big ones.

The thing that people don't often think about, though, is that an hour spent with acquaintances costs the same as an hour spent with good friends. Sixty minutes, either way, one hour with tremendous power behind it, and the other promising nothing beyond the superficial.

When examined through this lens, spending time with acquaintances is often a poor use of time. The alternative is just too positive to ignore. That's not to say that you can't make the best of that time and help others have a good time, just that there's a high cost to it.

Just as every tree begins as a seed, every close friendship begins as an acquaintance. Spending time with acquaintances who might become close friends someday is an excellent use of time. The trap that people fall into is when they hang out with acquaintances and friends with whom they'll never have a deeper relationship. Sometimes they do it out of loneliness, other times for superficial fun. Those are trade-offs that can be made, but it's important to know the cost.

Think very carefully about how you spend your social time. I'd say that one of the most significant indicators into how good someone's friend group is going to be in a few years is how high of a percentage of that time is spent with either close friends or people with the clear potential to become close friends.

When you have friends or acquaintances with whom you don't want a closer friendship, or who don't want a more intimate association with you, it's best to cease all effort to spend time with them. That doesn't mean to be friendly and kind to them, to make the best use of your time as well as theirs.

Treat Everyone Well

When I speak about cutting out acquaintances and being protective about how you spend your social time, it can come across as being cold and hostile. That's not the intention, though, and it's not how it translates in real life. As an inviolable rule, I believe in treating everyone well.

You have incomplete control over how you spend your time. You can try to maximize the time spent with good friends and people moving towards becoming good friends, but sometimes you'll be at a party with a different crowd than you'd choose, or you'll be in a line in the airport with people you didn't choose at all.

You ultimately control how you treat other people, unlike how you manage your time. In any given situation, you have the full agency to be friendly or unfriendly, cold or warm.

When you decide to treat someone well, you are creating goodwill and positive emotions out of nothing. Sometimes the effects of your manner will be small, but other times they'll have a massive impact on another person. You never know, and there's a lot of variances.

While you may have a good idea of how a close friend is feeling, you'll generally have less of an idea.

Smile a Little Bit

It doesn't hurt to smile. Every time you smile to other people, you will notice that they get relaxed and probably, smile back at you. Some scientists have conducted extensive research on whether there is a possible link between someone's mood and facial expressions. After years of researching, it was finally revealed that even faking a smile alone can trigger some positive feelings in you and also relieve some stress.

When combined with facial expressions, a smile can send a powerful message to the other party. So, you can try to get rid of your negativity by even faking a smile. No one will bother finding out whether your smile is genuine or fake as long as your intentions of breaking your negative thoughts are clear to you. If it doesn't come automatically, you can think of a funny moment that made you laugh a lot to induce a smile across your face.

You can imagine the effect created by someone smiling at you. Probably you may feel good within yourself and start smiling back at the person. A simple smile can change a tense situation and open up for everyone to approach you. This is a simple tactic that you can easily employ to win many people's hearts. But not everyone who smiles at you has good intentions. Always be aware of such people whenever you are at a social setup. Otherwise, a kind and genuine smile can lead you to establish your first friendship with someone you barely knew a few hours before your meeting.

Overcome Your Fear

Fear is part of our life but a critical factor that hinders progress. Sadly most of the negative thinkers have got some elements of horror in them, which leads to being pessimistic or judgmental for everything they encounter. A negative thinker is always scared of other people's progress, and this comes about because of fear.

When your fear and negativity pop right inside your head, you should choose to ignore them or stick on the path of truth as one way of overcoming your negative thoughts. Telling the truth will you give you more power and freedom to do what is right all the time. That is why there is a lot of freedom in knowing that every negative thought does not come from you.

Choose to be truthful and keep on moving forward with a lot of optimism, faith, and believe in you. Where there is fear, there no love, and where love is lacking, there is hatred. Therefore, you can overcome your fear first if you want to change your social life. Fear contributes more to negative thoughts, which, in turn, leads someone to start avoiding people for no reasons. Try to replace your fear with courage and see what happens next. Get rid of your fear and overcome your negative thoughts to have better social skills.

Chapter 8: Read Widely About Social Skills

Contrary to the common belief that reading makes people introverts, a new study reveals that reading widely can improve your social skills. The information contained in the reading materials can teach you a few tricks to help you in a social situation. Apart from that, there are volumes and volumes of books that are written to guide you on how to become a social person. After all, wide reading helps you to develop a firm foundation on which you can gradually start developing your skills as you enrich yourself with more knowledge. Before you grab your first copy to start reading on social skills, you can start by asking yourself the following helpful questions.

"How does reading widely improve social skills?"

There is no better way of acquiring knowledge than reading. Not just reading anything for the sake of it but reading quality material with vital information. The importance of text has been highly emphasized to have a positive impact on our way of thinking, analyzing concepts and answering questions. And of course, wide reading widely is often regarded as one of the most critical skills to overlap into our social situations as we interact with each other.

Social skills are part of our growth and development right from the time when we were just little boys and girls till getting into the advanced old age. As time passes, we find ourselves faced with different situations and given that we are the most advanced of the creations in the universe, we strive as much as we can to find a working solution to every challenge coming our way. What exactly is what distinguishes us from other animals? We are having that at the back of your mind; you can always harness your social skills so you may have a positive impact not only on your life but to someone else. Through social skills, you can achieve this goal and many more to come.

Reading widely on social skills is a vital step to discovering the right path into the realms of a social world. While we are establishing networks to get in touch with each other on the digital front, we're also becoming less and less connected by each passing moment. In other words, we are getting ourselves into what we can refer to us a virtual world. A world that exposes you to different situations and people without necessarily getting in touch physically. And the most affected groups of people are the children born and raised in this technically advanced era. More children are now being built in this changing and fast-paced environment, making them learn entirely new social skills. But there is no way we can abandon our traditions in favor of this emerging virtual world. At least we can help those growing up to integrate seamlessly into a physical, social society.

As children grow up and move on to the adulthood or the job market, they get exposed on the other side of the social world away from the digital front they are used to. That is when reality dawns on everyone, and learning appropriate methods of interacting socially at the tender age becomes even more critical. Reading books and any other relevant content becomes the only way to improve those social skills.

"Does reading improve concentration and patience?"

It is a well-known fact that reading widely improves focus as well as concentration not only in academics but in all aspects of life. Being focused is an essential part of your social interaction and a vital tool to help you improve your social skills.

If you are not sure about this, sit back and think about those relevant traits that dictate a good conversation. Of course, your mind will wander a little bit and bring you back to attributes such as the ability to give undivided attention, full concentration, being present in that moment, being patient till the other party finish their thought without interrupting them, and staying in the conversation. This may sound like a plot of a book, but these are the best attributes of reading widely if at all, you are looking forward to becoming a social person. Reading helps one to develop concentration and patience, making you better at conversations and conflict resolution.

"Does reading increase empathy?"

Reading is a part of learning and adopting helpful ideas. Through reading books, magazines, blogs, or even scientific journals, you get a better insight on how to relate to different situations and people. At the same time, reading can make you have that ability to get inside another person's mind and try to feel like them and understand their thoughts. This sounds like an impossible concept, but it works pretty perfectly for almost everybody. Explaining how this concept works is hard, especially for adults and even harder for children. Keep in mind that children are not yet born with the ability to be empathetic. They learn this incredible skill through interacting socially with their families, their peers, and the society in general. However, they can even get better by reading relevant books and any other recommended materials.

According to researchers, reading fictional books can help you get into the minds of other people, allow you to experience many challenges, get emotional and triumph over any adversity that comes alongside your favorite characters. All these happen as a result of getting immersed directly into another person's mind by stimulating systems in your brain that lead to the development of your ability to empathize with other people.

"Does reading widely enhance social problem-solving?"

Besides learning to empathize with other people, wide reading can provide you with an endless supply of the social interaction examples with which you can learn one or two effective tactics. How is this possible in the first place? Scenes full of dialogues can be a better platform to discover new conversational ideas. Such views will teach you how to handle any conflict arising between you and another person in various situations.

Also, they allow you to experience a broader range of emotions and moods that you are likely not to experience in your daily life. When you encounter these emotions and attitudes in a safer environment, you get a better chance to visualize how you might react in real life if a similar situation occurs. In other words, reading and imagining scenes with dialogues can prepare you adequately for future interactions. As a result, this makes your emotional development to be better-rounded and mature in every way possible. This is very helpful in a social situation, given that you will be able to enhance your social problem-solving naturally.

"Does reading provide you with topics for discussion?"

It is evident that when you read widely, you will be in a better position to find relevant topics of your discussion with someone. It is right to say that reading holds the gold standards for sparking thoughtful and mature talks no matter where you are or who you are engaging. Reading from different sources impact you with the right knowledge as well as providing you with topics of discussions. Some of those topics might not be common in your everyday conversation. Apart from that, these topics can aid you in logic thinking, improve your analytical skills and become perfect tools for group discussion.

"Does reading widely allow healthy emotional release?"

Reading is a very vital tool that can help you work through your emotions. Every word and phrase you read can entertain, uplift and elevate your mood. This is especially important and helpful in our ever-changing world today. As you know, the hustle and bustle of our daily lives can become stressful and tiring the mind, hence the need to find an immediate solution. The solution, however, lies in reading quietly to relax your mind and your body after a long day of running up and down.

Reading can liberate you from stress, anxiety, depression and also help you achieve that healthy emotional release leaving you relaxed and happier than before. This is equally vital when it comes to social interaction. You can only mingle and have meaningful conversations with other people when you are comfortable, relaxed and well-focused. Therefore, wide reading can as well enhance your social skills and make you an all-around person.

"Can reading widely improve your understanding?"

The more you read, the better you understand how different concepts are applied and how things work. Understanding how different things work plays a significant role in the way you and other people fit perfect in the grand scheme of all things. Through extensive reading, you can easily understand different people, different cultures, different societies, different places, and different beliefs.

By now, you know how different people are and that what is right for society may not work for another and vice versa. When you read widely and understand how to handle yourself in different situations, you can significantly improve your social skills.

At least you are fully aware of human intricate when it comes to behavior, actions, tastes, and preferences. Once you have all these factors at your fingertips, nothing should stand on your way from becoming a good decision maker to influence those in your social circle. With time you will get to realize that your knowledge of different people and life has improved so much that you can quickly get along with anyone despite their backgrounds. Just like how Matthew Effect states, "The rich get richer, while the poor get poorer," the same also goes with reading. In simple terms, widely reading will make you more vibrant and more abundant in knowledge, principles, and concepts that are vital in society in general. So, read widely to improve your understanding and later to inspire others through social interaction.

Books to Help Improve Your Social Skills

Luckily, there is more than enough written materials that can change the way you socialize with others. And books are a perfect example of rich sources of dispensable knowledge on how you can improve from being an ardent introvert to an overnight social person. Perhaps you may turn down this idea but be assured that reading can make a whole lot of differences in the way you carry yourself. That is why several authors from all walks of life have written books that can inspire, influence and eventually teaches you how you can easily make friends, communicate, meet people and interact well. Take a look at the following few examples of books that will sharpen your social skills:

"How to Win Friends and Influence People" by Dale Carnegie

The book, *"How to Win Friends and Influence People"* was written more than eight decades ago, and it is still regarded as one of the best-selling books on social skills. Since its first copy hit the bookshelves, many new editions of the same book have so far been released on the market. The most important part of the original advice is what matters the most to those looking to polish their social skills. Although the facts laid down in this excellent book are somehow anecdotal, you will find them very helpful and educative at the same time.

The author breaks down "How to Win Friends and Influence People" into sections that are understandable to those who want to take their social skills to the next level. Some of them are highlighted under the chapters: "Six Ways to Make People Like You" and "Fundamental Techniques for Handling People" and so on. The advice given here will definitely change your way of thinking and socializing.

"How to Talk to Anyone" by Leil Lowndes

This is one of the latest books that have taken the social world by storm. In fact, it is one of the books that contain the subtitle: "92 Little Tricks for Big Success in Relationships". The book has so far played a key role in improving social success for some readers. One of the reviews on the book reads. "This book can make you into a special person," and indeed that is absolutely true. You may give it a try and see how far you will go.

"Compelling People: The Hidden Qualities that Make Us Influential" by John Neffinger and Matthew Kohut

Neffinger and Kohut's *"Compelling People"* is a summary of many years of the research and experience put down on paper by the two authors. Their compelling thesis reads like this, "When we decide how we feel about someone, we are making not one judgment, but two. The criteria that count are what we call 'strength' and 'warmth'".

According to the explanation given, "strength" in this context means the person's ability to make things happen while "warmth" denotes the sense with which a person shares other people's feelings, views and interests. Understanding the two concepts is not a big deal, but the trick comes in implementing and applying them in real life as well as harnessing the power of their insight to your advantage.

"How to Instantly Connect with Anyone" by Leil Lowndes

Lowndes' "How to Instantly Connect with Anyone" is similar to her ***"How to Talk to Anyone"*** in terms of its structure, but the content and techniques are somehow different. This book helps you to implement what the author had previously expressed in her first book regarding relations.

The information contained in it is rich in making you become the best person socially. It takes you to step by step from the moment you meet someone all the way to establishing that much-needed connection within the shortest time possible. Reading it will open up your mind and give you an advantage over others on how to make you stand out from the crowd.

"How to Work a Room" by Susan RoAne

The book gives you helpful tips that can transform you from a dull person to a more charming character. It is evident that being charming will provide you with an excellent platform to showcase your social skills to others. In addition to that, charming people have no problem with establishing an instant link with other people, especially in a standard setup.

Even though *__How to Work a Room__* leans a little on the professional side, it also provides useful tips that you can apply when talking to different people at a networking event. Also, it goes as far as explaining how you can get along with others at weddings, parties or other social situations. Overall, the tips in this book can help you become an influential figure in a socializing crowd.

"What EVERYBODY is Saying" by Joe Navarro

This book is written by Joe-Navarro, an ex-FBI agent, and it is an excellent book for people to read to learn a few tricks that can transform them into social beings. The content of the book gives an insight into using your body language in a social situation.

Your body language can tell so much about you and at the same time, can portray your social skills to others. However, having good social skills is all about understanding emotions, thoughts and motives of those around you. It sounds even better to learn how to read and understand the body language of others, which is equally helpful.

"The How of Happiness" by Sonja Lyubomirsky

It is a well-known fact that people tend to get attracted to happy people. The best way to enhance your ability to relate to different people is just by starting from within. Once you understand your ability, you will be in a better position to influence others and make them want to relate to you.

This book contains vital information on several scientific studies pointing at what makes people happier than others and how that happiness can be translated into actionable steps. Lyubomirsky's ***"The How of Happiness"*** is by far one of the best books containing valuable information that can change your social life for the better.

"How to Win Friends and Influence People" by Dale Carnegie

This is a classic book for all the right reasons you may think of. Don't be discouraged by its title but flip the pages to discover useful tips that have actual meanings of being a social person. The book encourages you to take acting classes in a bid to get transformed from a shy person to a completely different person.

On the other hand, the book helps you to empathize with other people. In the actual sense, social skills don't just come naturally, but they are adopted through learning. Reading books exposes you to a learning process that is necessary to change your views and perspective on socialization.

"Talk like TED" by Carmine Gallo

This book uncovers nine common elements from TED talks. Also, it provides you with advice on how to adopt those nine common elements for the sake of improving your social life. The book goes as far as offering practical tips that are tailored towards improving your skills in public speaking.

If you are a reader looking to become better in public speaking, this is the best choice of a book for you. You will learn the proper format of making your speech and how to present it to the public while giving a captivating story that touches the minds and hearts of your audience.

"Antifragility: Things that Gain from Disorder" by Nassim Nicholas Taleb

The author focuses on composure and confidence as the two most essential skills in any effective communication. He goes further to provide the readers with a comprehensive guide on how one can become antifragile.

This book is quite helpful, and it will motivate you into finding out where you are most exposed. At the same time, it will help to identify where you can lose the most. Antifragile is highly recommended for those seeking knowledge that will make them grow from disaster to something more meaningful. At the end of reading it, you will have learned how to thrive from volatility, shock, and uncertainty.

Reading widely on how to improve your social skills will place you one step ahead of everyone in any social situation. What you will learn should help you harness your social skills, understand how to interact with others and know how to apply your newly acquired tips to make you stand among the rest.

Conclusion

Thank you so much for making it to the end of "***Improve Your Social Skills***." Let's hope the book was informative and able to give you all the necessary content to help achieve your goals. The fact that you are through with this book doesn't mean you should not venture a little further on the same topic. Let this be your stepping stone to expanding your scope and the only way to discovering your full potential.

Now that you have this information at your fingertips, your next step should be getting out of your comfort zone and starting to apply what you've learned so far. Use that information wisely not only to help transform your social ways but, especially, to bring positive changes to others. What is important now is to understand that you are still at your initial stages of a learning process; hence, the need to pay close attention to every detail.

Naturally, it gets much more comfortable when tasks are broken down into smaller sections with individual deadlines. This will give you a greater chance of accomplishing your mission more systematically. The primary objective here is to see you make through to the highest levels of your society with your social skills. In the end, you will look back and feel great for having accomplished a critical task in your life.

Finally, if you found the information contained in this book useful to you, a review is always appreciated!